はしがき

　本書は第一学習社発行の英語教科書「CREATIVE English Communication Ⅲ」に完全準拠したノートです。各見開き 2 ページで，主に教科書本文の予習や授業傍用での使用に役立つよう工夫しました。

CONTENTS

本書の構成と利用法

　本書は教科書本文を完全に理解するための学習の導きをしています。本書を最大限に活用して，教科書本文の理解を深めましょう。

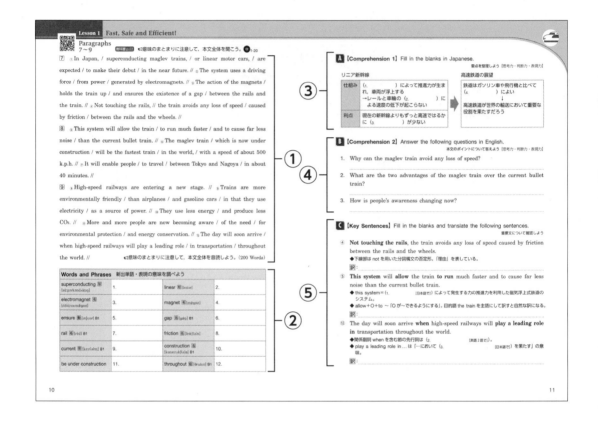

① 教科書本文

　意味のまとまりごとにスラッシュ（/）を入れました。ここで示した意味のまとまりを意識しながら音読しましょう。また学習がしやすいよう，一文ずつ番号を付けました。上部の二次元コードは本文音声のリスニングや音読に使用できる「スピーキング・トレーナー」にリンクしています。右ページに詳しい解説があります。

　　※本文中の グレーのマーカー は，教科書では印字されておらず，音声としてのみ配信している部分であることを示します。

　　※ ●₀₀は，生徒用音声CD（別売）のディスク番号とトラック番号を示します。

② Words and Phrases

　新出単語・表現の意味を調べて，意味を日本語で記入しましょう。単語の品詞と発音記号も示しました。A1～B2は，CEFR-Jでのレベルを示します。色の付いた単語は，読んで意味がわかるだけでなく，表現活動でも使えるようにしておきたい語です。

　『CEFR-J Wordlist Version 1.6』東京外国語大学投野由紀夫研究室.
　（URL: http://cefr-j.org/download.html より2021年2月ダウンロード）

③ **A**問 ────────────────────────────

　図表を日本語で完成させることで本文の理解を深める問題です。地図・グラフなど，パートごとにさまざまな形の図表を完成させます。

④ **B**問 ────────────────────────────

　教科書本文に関連する英語の質問に対し，英語で答える問題です。教科書の **Q** とは別の問題としています。**A**問で完成させた図表がヒントになる問題も含まれています。

⑤ **C**問 ────────────────────────────

　教科書の各文で，文法事項やリーディングスキルに関連したもの，また文構造が複雑なものや指示語を含むものなどを重要文と位置づけ，解説を加えました。解説を日本語や英語で完成させ，和訳をする問題です。

Web コンテンツ

スピーキング・トレーナー

本文の音声データ無料配信，音読用のボイスレコーダーが使用できます。
https://dg-w.jp/b/e8f0014

音声データ配信

・音声データを無料でダウンロード，または再生ができます。音声ファイルは MP3形式，一括ダウンロードは ZIP 形式になっております。

　＊アップしてある音声データは著作権法で保護されています。音声データの利用は個人が私的に利用する場合に限られます。データを第三者に提供・販売することはできません。

ボイスレコーダー　　アクセスキー：h6aeh

・音読の学習効果をさらに高めるために，自分の発話の録音ができるボイスレコーダーを用意しました。PC やスマートフォンからご利用できます。
　ボイスレコーダーの使用にはユーザー ID とパスワードが必要です。ID とパスワードを自分で設定（半角英数字5文字以上）して，利用を開始してください。

メモ欄

ID	
パスワード	

　＊ ID とパスワードは紛失しないようにしてください。万が一紛失した場合は，それまでに記録された学習履歴がすべて参照できなくなります。復元はできませんので，ご注意ください。
　＊正常に動作しない場合は「ヘルプ」→「動作要件」をご確認ください。

CHECK 教科書p.6 📢意味のまとまりに注意して，本文全体を聞こう。 ◎1-2

①Fully electric cars are increasing / around the world. // ②Before they came into the market, / hybrid cars had gained in popularity. //

③It has been more than a quarter of a century / since the first consumer hybrid car made its debut / in 1997, / and there are an increasing number of hybrid cars / on the market / these days. // ④Hybrid means a combination / of two different things. // ⑤A hybrid car is one / that uses two different energy sources / to maximize efficiency. // ⑥The reason for its growing popularity is / that it has several advantages / over a conventional car / powered by gasoline. // ⑦For example, / hybrid cars produce less emissions / and use less gasoline / by making good use / of an engine / and an electric motor. // ⑧They use one of them / or both / depending on driving conditions. // ⑨When the gasoline engine needs power, / it also uses an electric motor / so that it uses less gasoline. // ⑩On the other hand, / when the car is braking, / the energy is used / to charge the batteries. // ⑪As a result, / the longer the travel distance is, / the better the fuel efficiency tends to be. // ⑫In addition, / taxes on hybrid cars / have been cut / in recent years. // ⑬A hybrid car will offer greater economy, / tax benefits, / and fewer emissions / than a conventional car. // ⑭Therefore, / it is gaining strong support / from the public now. //

📢意味のまとまりに注意して，本文全体を音読しよう。（199 Words）

Words　新出単語の意味を調べよう			
combination 名 [kɑ̀(:)mbɪnéɪʃ(ə)n] B1	1.	efficiency 名[ɪfíʃ(ə)nsi] B1	2.
conventional 形 [kənvénʃ(ə)n(ə)l] B2	3.	gasoline 名[ɡǽsəliːn]	4.
emission 名[ɪmíʃ(ə)n]	5.	motor 名[móʊtər] B1	6.
brake 動[bréɪk] A2	7.	fuel 名[fjúːəl] B1	8.
tax 名[tǽks] B1	9.	offer 動[ɔ́ːfər] A2	10.

A 【Comprehension 1】 Fill in the blanks in Japanese.

ハイブリッド車
登場：(1.　　　　　　　) 年 ガソリン車より… ・(2.　　　　　　　) が少ない。 ・(3.　　　　　　　) の使用量が少ない。 ・移動距離が長いほど (4.　　　　　　　) がよくなる傾向がある。 ・近年では (5.　　　　　) が控除される。 　　　　　　　　　　　結果，ハイブリッド車は人々の支持を得ている。

B 【Comprehension 2】 Answer the following questions in English.

本文のポイントについて答えよう【思考力・判断力・表現力】

1. What does the word "hybrid" originally mean?

2. When do the batteries in hybrid cars charge?

3. What are the three benefits that a hybrid car may offer to the owner?

C 【Key Sentences】 Fill in the blanks and translate the following sentences.

重要文について確認しよう【知識・技能】【思考力・判断力・表現力】

② Before **they** came into the market, hybrid cars **had gained** in popularity.
   ◆ they＝(1.　　　　　　　　　[英語3語で])。
   ◆過去完了形 had gained は大過去の用法。before の節よりも主節のほうが以前であることを表す。
   ◆ gain in ... 「…を徐々に増す」。
   訳：

⑤ A hybrid car is one that uses **two different energy sources** to maximize efficiency.
   ◆この文の two different energy sources は (2.　　　　　[日本語で]) と (3.　　　　　[日本語で]) であると推測できる。
   ◆ to maximize efficiency は目的のほか，結果と解釈することもできる。
   訳：

⑭ **Therefore**, it is gaining strong support from the public now.
   ◆ therefore は (4.　　　　　[日本語で]) を表すディスコースマーカー。その原因を簡潔に表す一文は，(5.　　　　　[英語一文で])。
   訳：

TRY 教科書p.8-p.9 🔊意味のまとまりに注意して，本文全体を聞こう。 ◎1-4・6

A ①There is a perfectly good word / for "no" / in the Japanese language, / but it is seldom used. // ②"Yes," / on the other hand, / is heard / all the time. // ③This does not mean, / however, / that the Japanese do not say "no." // ④In fact, / they say it / quite often, / even if what they have said sounds like "yes" / to newcomers. //

⑤For many generations / the Japanese were conditioned / to avoid blunt responses and confrontations / of any kind. // ⑥Since "no" is often confrontational, / the Japanese do not like / to come right out / and say it. //

⑦The Japanese have also been almost as uncomfortable with "yes" / as they have been with "no." // ⑧"Yes" could, / and often did, / lead to new commitments and responsibilities. // ⑨As a result, / "yes" gradually came to be synonymous / with "Yes, / I heard you" / or "Yes, / I am listening," / ceasing to mean / "Yes, / I agree with you." //

⑩Thus / it happened / in Japan / that the use of "yes" and "no" / became very subtle, / requiring the hearer / to be exceptionally skilled / in interpreting what the speaker meant. // ⑪The main reason for this / was the overriding need / to maintain harmony, / and the importance of self-preservation. //

B ①Children / in developing countries work / for a variety of reasons; / the most common reason / is poverty. // ②Children work / so that they and their families can survive. // ③Though these children are not paid well, / their families are so poor / that they still serve / as major contributors / to family income. // ④For instance, / children in poor families / in Paraguay / contribute almost 25 percent / of the total household income. //

⑤In developing countries, / rural-to-urban migration is another cause of child labor. // ⑥In the last 40 years, / more and more people have migrated / from the country / to the city. // ⑦In 1950, / just 17 percent of the population / of the developing world / lived in urban areas. // ⑧This figure increased / to 40 percent / by the year 2000. // ⑨It will probably reach 57 percent / by the year 2030. // ⑩Poor families / who move to the cities / usually do not find enough work. // ⑪Moving to the cities forces families / into poverty, / and poverty forces parents / to send children / to work. //

🔊意味のまとまりに注意して，本文全体を音読しよう。(A: 189 Words   B: 159 Words)

Words and Phrases 新出単語・表現の意味を調べよう			
newcomer 名 [njúːkʌmər] B1	1.	be conditioned to ～	2.
blunt 形 [blʌ́nt]	3.	response 名 [rɪspá(ː)ns] A2	4.

confrontation 名 [kà(:)nfrʌntéɪʃ(ə)n]	5.	confrontational 形 [kà(:)nfrʌntéɪʃ(ə)n(ə)l]	6.
come right out and say …	7.	commitment 名 [kəmítmənt] A2	8.
gradually 副 [grǽdʒu(ə)li] A2	9.	synonymous 形 [sɪná(:)nəməs]	10.
cease 動 [síːs] B2	11.	thus 副 [ðʌ́s] B1	12.
hearer 名 [híərər]	13.	exceptionally 副 [ɪksépʃ(ə)n(ə)li] B2	14.
overriding 形 [òuvərráɪdɪŋ]	15.	self-preservation 名 [sèlfprèzərvéɪʃ(ə)n]	16.
serve as …	17.	contributor 名 [kəntríbjətər]	18.
Paraguay [pǽrəgwàɪ]	19.	rural 形 [rúər(ə)l] B2	20.
urban 形 [ə́ːrb(ə)n] B2	21.	migration 名 [maɪgréɪʃ(ə)n] B2	22.
labor 名 [léɪbər] A2	23.	migrate 動 [máɪgreɪt]	24.
force … to ～	25.		

A 【Comprehension 1】 Fill in the blanks in Japanese.

要点を整理しよう【思考力・判断力・表現力】

A　タイトル「日本人の『ノー』」	B　タイトル「(3.　　　　　　　　　　)」
日本人は「ノー」とめったに言わない。「イエス」と聞こえるような場合にも，実際には「ノー」と言っている場合がある。【理由】日本人は（1.　　　　　　　）や（2.　　　　　　　）を避けるよう訓練されているから。調和を保つ必要性，自己防衛の重要性。	発展途上国の子供たちが働くのは主に（4.　　　　　　　）のため。パラグアイの貧困家庭の子供は家計の総収入の約（5.　　　　）パーセントに寄与している。農村から都市への移動も理由のひとつ。都市に移住すると仕事がなく，家族は（4.　　　　　　　）になる。

B 【Comprehension 2】 Answer the following questions in English.

本文のポイントについて答えよう【思考力・判断力・表現力】

1.　Why don't Japanese like to come right out and say "no"?

2.　Why do parents in developing countries send their children to work?

CHECK 教科書p.10 ◀意味のまとまりに注意して，本文全体を聞こう。 ◎1-8

①People have lived / with domesticated animals / for thousands of years. // ②Typical examples / include sheep, / goats, / pigs, / horses and chickens, / but dogs have been around / with us / longer than any other animal. // ③Some scientists argue / that dogs started moving around / with humans / about 20,000 years ago. // ④This is probably / why many people believe / "a dog is human's best friend." // ⑤However, / it is actually said / that there are more cats / in Japan / than dogs nowadays. // ⑥Cats have also been domesticated / for a long time / since around 7,500 BC. //

⑦Japan is sometimes described / as a country / in which pets outnumber children. // ⑧According to the Japan Pet Food Association, / there are about 18 million cats and dogs, / while there are just around 15 million children / under the age of 15. // ⑨This trend is likely to continue / in the future. //

◀意味のまとまりに注意して，本文全体を音読しよう。（135 Words）

Words and Phrases 新出単語・表現の意味を調べよう			
thousands of ...	1.	domesticated 形 [dəméstɪkèɪtɪd]	2.
argue 動 [ɑ́ːrgjuː] A2	3.	describe A as B	4.
outnumber 動 [àʊtnʌ́mbər]	5.	association 名 [əsòʊsiéɪʃ(ə)n] A2	6.

A 【Comprehension 1】 Fill in the blanks in Japanese.

約20,000年前	紀元前7500年ころ	現代
(1.) と人類が いっしょに動き始める。	人類が (2.) を飼い慣らし始める。	15歳未満の子供の人口： 約 (3.) 人 犬猫の飼育頭数 約 (4.) 匹

B 【Comprehension 2】 Answer the following questions in English.

1. What animal has been around with us for the longest time?

   ----

2. In Japan, which is said to be larger in number, dogs or cats?

   ----

3. What is "a country in which pets outnumber children"?

C 【Key Sentences】 Fill in the blanks and translate the following sentences.

④ **This** is probably **why** many people believe "a dog is human's best friend."

◆ This＝(1.   [日本語で])。

◆ this is why ... は「そういうわけで…」の意味。why は関係副詞。理由が先に示される。

訳：--

⑤ However, **it is** actually **said that** there are more cats in Japan than dogs nowadays.

◆ it is said that ... は「…と言われている」の意味。it は that-節を導くためのもので，具体的な意味をもたない。

訳：--

⑦ Japan is sometimes described as <u>a country</u> (**in which** pets outnumber children).

◆関係詞が前置詞の目的語になる場合〈先行詞＋前置詞＋関係代名詞〉の語順になる。pets outnumber children in a country の関係がある。

◆この文の場合，in which を (2.   [英語1語で]) で置きかえることができる。

訳：--

TRY 教科書 p.12 ◁意味のまとまりに注意して，本文全体を聞こう。 1-10

①You've heard / about a policy change / in your city. // ②You are reading / the discussions about the policy / in an online forum. //

③Subject: / Abolishment of Community Buses //　　　　〈Posted on 19 December〉

④To whom it may concern, /

⑤I am posting / to ask you / to continue the service of community buses / between Sakura Village / and the city center. // ⑥I heard / that the city is going to abolish the service / next September. //

⑦My parents are both over 80 years old, / living on their own / in the village. // ⑧They don't drive / and frequently use community buses / to go shopping / in the city center. // ⑨I know / the amount of money being made / on the buses / is declining, / but I believe / the service is essential / for older people / in the village / like my parents. // ⑩Although the number of people using the service / seems to have dropped / recently, / I believe / there is still a possibility / of an increase / in users / because the city's population is aging / fast. // ⑪I would like your reconsideration. //

⑫Regards, /

⑬Martin Jones //

⑭Dear Martin, //　　　　〈Posted on 20 December〉

⑮Thank you / for your inquiry. // ⑯It was actually a tough decision / for us / to abolish the community buses. // ⑰Due to a lack of financial sources, / however, / we had to carry out / a review of local services / as a whole / and look carefully / at the unprofitable ones, / including the community buses. // ⑱The number of bus users has dropped / by 39% / since 2010. // ⑲I'm sorry / to have to say it, / but unless we can expect / an increase / in users, / it will be difficult / to withdraw the decision / to abolish the buses. //

⑳Thank you very much / for your understanding. //

㉑Sincerely, /

㉒Miho Yamaguchi //

㉓City Planning Division //

◁意味のまとまりに注意して，本文全体を音読しよう。（246 Words）

Words and Phrases	新出単語・表現の意味を調べよう		
policy 名 [pá(:)ləsi] B1	1.	forum 名 [fɔ́:rəm]	2.
abolishment 名 [əbá(:)lɪʃmənt]	3.	abolish 動 [əbá(:)lɪʃ] B2	4.
be essential for …	5.	reconsideration 名 [rì:kənsìdəréɪʃ(ə)n]	6.
regard 名 [rɪgá:rd] B2	7.	inquiry 名 [ínkwəri] B1	8.
a lack of …	9.	unprofitable 形 [ʌnprá(:)fətəb(ə)l]	10.
unless 接 [ənlés] B1	11.	withdraw 動 [wɪðdrɔ́:] B2	12.
division 名 [dɪvíʒ(ə)n] B2	13.		

A 【Comprehension 1】 Fill in the blanks in Japanese.

要点を整理しよう【思考力・判断力・表現力】

マーティン・ジョーンズ

コミュニティバスの運行を
(1.　　　　) させたい。
【理由】
・高齢の両親は車を運転できず，
　バスを利用する。
【主張の根拠】
・市の (2.　　　　) が急速に
　進んでおり，バスの利用者が
　増える可能性がある。

都市計画課

コミュニティバスの運行を
(3.　　　　) したい。
【理由】
・財源不足のため地域サービス
　全体の見直しをしている。
【主張の根拠】
・バスの利用者は (4.　　　　)
　年から (5.　　　　) パーセ
　ント減少している。

B 【Comprehension 2】 Answer the following questions in English.

本文のポイントについて答えよう【思考力・判断力・表現力】

1. Why did Martin post his opinion on the online forum?

2. How many days did it take Miho to answer Martin's request?

3. What could cause the city to withdraw the decision to abolish the buses?

CHECK 教科書 p.14 ◀意味のまとまりに注意して，本文全体を聞こう。 ◎1-12・13

A ①Vincent van Gogh (1853-90) //

②Vincent van Gogh was a Dutch painter / who went to live / in southern France / and who helped develop the style / of Post-Impressionism. // ③His paintings / typically use bright colors / and have thick lines of paint / in circular patterns, / and the most famous ones include Sunflowers and Irises. // ④Although he wasn't famous / during his lifetime, / today / he is considered / one of the greatest / and most influential artists / of his time. // ⑤His paintings are now extremely valuable / and are sold / for very high prices. //

B [...]

⑥One of the reasons / why I'm now without a position, / why I've been without a position / for years, / is quite simply because I have different ideas / from these gentlemen / who give positions / to individuals / who think like them. //

⑦It's not a simple matter / of appearance, / it's something / more serious / than that, / I assure you. //

[...]

⑧Well, / that's not quite how it is; / what has changed is / that my life was less difficult / then / and my future less dark, / but as far as my inner self, / as far as my way of seeing and thinking are concerned, / they haven't changed. // ⑨But if / in fact / there were a change, / it's that now I think / and I believe / and I love / more seriously / what then, / too, / I already thought, / I believed and I loved. //

[...]

⑩Letter to Theo van Gogh. // ⑪June 1880 //

◀意味のまとまりに注意して，本文全体を音読しよう。 (223 Words)

Words and Phrases 新出単語・表現の意味を調べよう			
Vincent van Gogh [víns(ə)nt væn góu]	ヴィンセント・ヴァン・ゴッホ	Post-Impressionism [póustɪmpréʃ(ə)nìzm]	後期印象派
typically 副 [típɪk(ə)li] B1	1.	circular 形 [sə́:rkjələr] B1	2.
iris 名 [áɪ(ə)rɪs]	3.	lifetime 名 [láɪftàɪm] B2	4.
extremely 副 [ɪkstríːmli] A2	5.	valuable 形 [vǽljəb(ə)l] B1	6.
position 名 [pəzíʃ(ə)n] A2	7.	assure 動 [əʃúər] B2	8.

inner 形 [ínər] A2	9.	as far as … is concerned	10.
Theo [θíːou]	テオ		

A 【Comprehension 1】 Fill in the blanks in Japanese.

要点を整理しよう【思考力・判断力・表現力】

【辞書】ヴィンセント・ヴァン・ゴッホ	ゴッホの手紙
・ゴッホは南フランスに渡った（1.　　　）の画家 ・後期印象派のスタイルを確立 ・代表作：『ひまわり』『アイリス』 ・(2.　　　　　) は有名ではなかった。 ・ゴッホの絵画は現在では価値が高い。	・ゴッホが役職に就けていない理由 　→役職を与える人と（3.　　　）が違う。 ・自分の内面，ものの見方，考え方は変わっていない。 ・自分が信じ愛するものに対してより深い思いを抱くようになった。

B 【Comprehension 2】 Answer the following questions in English.

本文のポイントについて答えよう【思考力・判断力・表現力】

1. When did van Gogh become famous?

　　　　　　　　　　　　　　　　　　　　　　　

2. Who did van Gogh write to in June 1880?

　　　　　　　　　　　　　　　　　　　　　　　

C 【Key Sentences】 Translate the following sentences.

重要文について確認しよう【知識・技能】【思考力・判断力・表現力】

⑥ …I have different ideas from these gentlemen (**who** give positions to individuals (**who** think like **them**)).

◆関係詞節中の単語がさらに関係詞で修飾されている。
◆ like は前置詞で「…と同じように」の意味。them は these gentlemen を指す。

訳：

⑨ But if in fact there **were** a change, **it's** that now I think and I believe and I love more seriously what 〈then, too, 〉 I already thought, I believed and I loved.

◆ were は仮定法過去。主節に would は使われていないが，「もし変化が起きているのだとしたら」の意味。
◆ it は a change を指す。it is that の S＋V＋C の構文で，補語に that-節がきている。
◆ what I already thought, I believed and I loved が 3 つの動詞すべての目的語。

訳：

TRY 教科書 p.16 📢意味のまとまりに注意して，本文全体を聞こう。 ◎ 1-15・16

①You are studying / about sea turtles. // ②You found two articles / about them. //

③Sea Turtle //

④Sea turtles are one of the oldest kinds of animals. // ⑤They have been around / for over 100 million years. // ⑥They are generally larger / than land turtles. // ⑦Some sea turtles are huge. // ⑧They weigh / up to 400 pounds / (180 kilograms). // ⑨Large sea turtles can swim / up to 5.8 miles / (9.3 kilometers) / per hour. // ⑩Sea turtles live / in the deep ocean / most of the year. // ⑪For this reason, / scientists do not know / much about their behavior. // ⑫But they know / that sea turtles move around / a lot / to find food. // ⑬Sea turtles can travel / hundreds or thousands of miles / every year. // ⑭Some kinds of sea turtles eat / only plants. // ⑮Others eat plants, / shellfish, / or other sea animals. //

⑯Sea Turtle Conservation Program //

⑰The number of sea turtles has been decreasing / worldwide / due to human influences. // ⑱Chemicals and pollution of the water / from trash / cause health problems / for sea turtles. // ⑲Ingestion of fishing nets, / lines and hooks are other dangers. // ⑳Sea turtles caught in fishing nets / cannot reach the surface / to breathe. // ㉑Overdeveloped coastal areas / have destroyed the area / of their natural nesting environment / and increased lighting misguides baby turtles / and nesting mothers. // ㉒Especially / during the mating, / nesting, / and hatching seasons, / people need / to be careful / as sea turtles can be mostly found at / or just below the surface / in coastal waters. // ㉓Only 0.1 percent of baby turtles / that enter the ocean will survive / and become adults. // ㉔This is due to all the natural / and human-made dangers / they face. // ㉕For these reasons, / all sea turtle species should be protected. //

📢意味のまとまりに注意して，本文全体を音読しよう。(256 Words)

Words 新出単語の意味を調べよう			
pound 名 [páund] B1	1.	trash 名 [trǽʃ] B1	2.
ingestion 名 [ɪndʒéstʃ(ə)n]	3.	hook 名 [húk] B2	4.
overdeveloped 形 [òuvərdɪvéləpt]	5.	coastal 形 [kóust(ə)l] B1	6.

lighting 名[láɪtɪŋ] B2	7.	misguide 動[mɪsgáɪd]	8.
mate 動[méɪt]	9.	hatch 動[hǽtʃ]	10.

A 【Comprehension 1】 Fill in the blanks in Japanese.　要点を整理しよう【思考力・判断力・表現力】

ウミガメの紹介	ウミガメ保護プログラム
・１億年以上前から存在している。 ・大きいものは体重（1.　　　　）ポンド。 ・一年の大半を（2.　　　　）で過ごす。 ・植物だけを食べる種，ほかの海洋生物を食べる種がいる。	・ウミガメが減少している。 　→水質汚染　→漁網や釣り糸，釣り針 　→過度に開発された沿岸の地域 ・海に入ったウミガメのうち，生き残って成体になるのは（3.　　　　）パーセント。 　→自然による危険のほか，（4.　　　　）による危険のため。

B 【Comprehension 2】 Answer the following questions in English.

本文のポイントについて答えよう【思考力・判断力・表現力】

1. Why do scientists know little about sea turtles' behavior?

---

2. Where can sea turtles be found during their mating, nesting, and hatching seasons?

C 【Key Sentences】 Translate the following sentences.

重要文について確認しよう【知識・技能】【思考力・判断力・表現力】

㉑ Overdeveloped coastal areas (S) have destroyed (V) the area of their natural nesting environment (O) and increased lighting (S) misguides (V) baby turtles and nesting mothers (O).

◆2つのS＋V＋Oの文が and でつながれている。increased と nesting はいずれも分詞の形容詞用法。
◆have destroyed は現在完了形の完了用法。misguides は現在の状態を表す現在形。
訳：

㉒ ..., people need to be careful **as** sea turtles can be mostly found **at or just below** the surface in coastal waters.

◆as は理由を表す接続詞。注意が必要な理由を表している。
◆at or just below は，at と below の2つの前置詞を並列している。
訳：

15

Paragraphs 1〜3

教科書 p.20　🔊意味のまとまりに注意して，本文全体を聞こう。　◎1-18

①Japan is now constructing / a maglev train system / between Tokyo and Nagoya. // ②This train system is based / on advanced bullet train technology / developed in Japan. //

1　③The Shinkansen, / Japan's bullet trains, / zoomed onto the railway scene / on October 1, 1964. // ④It was just nine days / before the Tokyo Olympic Games began. // ⑤The Hikari, / then the fastest train, / shrank travel time / between Tokyo and Osaka / to less than half / of what it was previously. // ⑥Now the network has expanded / to over 3,000 kilometers of lines. //

2　⑦The Shinkansen was originally constructed / to reinforce the transportation capacity / of the Tokaido Line of Japanese National Railways, / in order to meet the needs / of rapid economic growth. // ⑧Since then, / the railway network / has played an important role / in the development of Japan. //

3　⑨The Japanese bullet train was the first high-speed railway system / in the world. // ⑩It was also a symbol / of Japan's recovery / from the devastation / of World War II. // ⑪Even today, / it remains one of the fastest train networks / in the world / and shows the highly-developed train technology / of Japan. // ⑫The Shinkansen has demonstrated / the importance and advantages / of high-speed railways. // ⑬Its success has had a great influence / on other railways / in the world. // ⑭Many countries are now constructing / and expanding high-speed railway networks. //　🔊意味のまとまりに注意して，本文全体を音読しよう。(167 Words)

Words and Phrases 新出単語・表現の意味を調べよう			
construct 動 [kənstrʌ́kt] B1	1.	maglev 名 [mǽglèv]	2.
bullet 名 [búlɪt] B1	3.	zoom 動 [zúːm]	4.
zoom onto ...	5.	railway 名 [réɪlwèɪ] B1	6.
shrank 動 [ʃrǽŋk] B2	shrink の過去形	shrink 動 [ʃríŋk] B2	7.
shrink A to B	8.	previously 副 [príːviəsli] B2	9.
network 名 [nétwə̀ːrk] B1	10.	expand 動 [ɪkspǽnd] B1	11.

capacity 名 [kəpǽsəti] B1	12.		rapid 形 [rǽpɪd] B1	13. .
recovery 名 [rɪkʌ́v(ə)ri] B1	14.		devastation 名 [dèvəstéɪʃ(ə)n]	15.
demonstrate 動 [démənstrèɪt] B1	16.			

A 【Comprehension 1】 Fill in the blanks in Japanese.

要点を整理しよう【思考力・判断力・表現力】

新幹線とは

開業	(1.　　　　　　) 年10月１日 →東京・大阪間の移動時間が（2.　　　　　　）に短縮
目的	(3.　　　　　　　　) で増加した東海道線の輸送力を（4.　　　　　　）するため
効果	(5.　　　　　　) の重要性と利点を示した →多くの国々の（5.　　　　　　）網建設や拡大につながっている

B 【Comprehension 2】 Answer the following questions in English.

本文のポイントについて答えよう【思考力・判断力・表現力】

1. What is the English name for the Shinkansen?

   ....

2. What was the original aim of the construction of the Shinkansen?

   ....

C 【Key Sentences】 Fill in the blanks and translate the following sentences.

重要文について確認しよう【知識・技能】【思考力・判断力・表現力】

⑤ The Hikari, <u>then the fastest train</u>, shrank travel time between Tokyo and Osaka to less than half of **what it was** previously.

   ◆ then the fastest train は「(1.　　　　　　[日本語で]）の最速列車」の意味。
   ◆ what ... was は「過去の…」という意味。it＝(2.　　　　　　[英語２語で]) between Tokyo and Osaka。
   訳 : ....

   ....

⑦ The Shinkansen was originally constructed **to reinforce** the transportation capacity of the Tokaido Line of Japanese National Railways, **in order to** meet the needs of rapid economic growth.

   ◆ to ～は「～するために」（目的）。in order to ～は「目的」の意味をより明確に表す。
   訳 : ....

   ....

Paragraphs 4〜6　教科書 p.21　◖意味のまとまりに注意して，本文全体を聞こう。◎1-20

4 　①The Tokaido Shinkansen is one of the world's busiest high-speed lines. // ②In 2017, / it carried / as many as 465,600 passengers / on 368 trains / per day / at time intervals of just three to six minutes. // ③In short, / the Japanese bullet train is an effective means / of high-speed and high-frequency mass transportation. //

5 　④Japan has geological conditions / unsuitable for bullet trains. // ⑤Mountainous terrain / with only small plain areas / has made it difficult / to extend the tracks / for high-speed railways. // ⑥Various other factors, / such as frequent earthquakes, / many volcanic mountains, / typhoons in summer and autumn, / and heavy snows in winter / have threatened the safe and accurate operation / of the trains. //

6 　⑦With all these disadvantages, / the Shinkansen deserves great praise / for having the highest level / of safety and efficiency / in the world. // ⑧The service has continued / to work well over the decades. // ⑨According to Central Japan Railway, / the average delay from schedule / per train / is an amazingly low 36 seconds. // ⑩It has maintained a record / of no passenger fatalities / resulting from train accidents / since its debut. // ⑪The Shinkansen stands / as a global symbol / of Japanese technological innovation / that has been studied / by many other countries. //　　　◖意味のまとまりに注意して，本文全体を音読しよう。(190 Words)

Words and Phrases　新出単語・表現の意味を調べよう			
passenger 名 [pǽsɪn(d)ʒər] A2	1.	interval 名 [íntərv(ə)l] B1	2.
in short	3.	effective 形 [ɪféktɪv] B1	4.
frequency 名 [fríːkwənsi] B1	5.	mass 形 [mǽs] B1	6.
geological 形 [dʒìːəlá(:)dʒɪk(ə)l]	7.	unsuitable 形 [ʌnsúːtəb(ə)l] B2	8.
be unsuitable for …	9.	mountainous 形 [máʊnt(ə)nəs]	10.
terrain 名 [təréɪn]	11.	factor 名 [fǽktər] B2	12.
frequent 形 [fríːkwənt] B1	13.	accurate 形 [ǽkjərət] B1	14.

operation 名 [à(:)pəréɪʃ(ə)n] B1	15.	with all …	16.
disadvantage 名 [dìsədvǽntɪdʒ] A2	17.	deserve 動 [dɪzə́:rv] B1	18.
schedule 名 [skédʒuːl] A2	19.	fatality 名 [feɪtǽləti]	20.

A 【**Comprehension 1**】 Fill in the blanks in Japanese. 要点を整理しよう【思考力・判断力・表現力】

日本の新幹線：高速・高頻度の（1.　　　　　　　　　）をする効果的な手段

新幹線にとっての不利な条件 ・（2.　　　）が多い地形 　→線路を広げにくい ・地震・火山・台風・大雪 　→安全で（3.　　　）な運行に支障	高い安全性と効率性 ・定時からの（4.　　　）が極めて少ない ・列車事故による乗客の（5.　　　　　　　）が 　発生していない 　→日本の技術革新の世界的な象徴

B 【**Comprehension 2**】 Answer the following questions in English.

本文のポイントについて答えよう【思考力・判断力・表現力】

1. How many trains carried their passengers per day on the Tokaido Shinkansen in 2017?

   ----

2. What factors have threatened the safe and accurate operation of the Shinkansen trains?

   ----

3. How many Shinkansen passengers have been killed in train accidents?

C 【**Key Sentences**】 Fill in the blanks and translate the following sentences.

重要文について確認しよう【知識・技能】【思考力・判断力・表現力】

② In 2017, **it** carried **as many as** 465,600 passengers on 368 trains per day at time intervals of just three to six minutes.

　◆ it＝(1.　　　　　　　　　　　　　[英語3語で]）

　◆ as many as に数を表す表現が続くと，「…もの（多くの）」というように，数が多いことを強調する。

　訳 : --

　　--

⑤ Mountainous terrain (**with** only small plain areas) has made **it** difficult to extend the tracks for high-speed railways.

　◆ it＝(2.　　　　　　　　　　　　　　　　[英語7語で]）

　訳 : --

　　--

Paragraphs 7〜9

教科書 p.22 ◀意味のまとまりに注意して，本文全体を聞こう。1-22

[7] ①In Japan, / superconducting maglev trains, / or linear motor cars, / are expected / to make their debut / in the near future. // ②The system uses a driving force / from power / generated by electromagnets. // ③The action of the magnets / holds the train up / and ensures the existence of a gap / between the rails and the train. // ④Not touching the rails, / the train avoids any loss of speed / caused by friction / between the rails and the wheels. //

[8] ⑤This system will allow the train / to run much faster / and to cause far less noise / than the current bullet train. // ⑥The maglev train / which is now under construction / will be the fastest train / in the world, / with a speed of about 500 k.p.h. // ⑦It will enable people / to travel / between Tokyo and Nagoya / in about 40 minutes. //

[9] ⑧High-speed railways are entering a new stage. // ⑨Trains are more environmentally friendly / than airplanes / and gasoline cars / in that they use electricity / as a source of power. // ⑩They use less energy / and produce less CO_2. // ⑪More and more people are now becoming aware / of the need / for environmental protection / and energy conservation. // ⑫The day will soon arrive / when high-speed railways will play a leading role / in transportation / throughout the world. //

◀意味のまとまりに注意して，本文全体を音読しよう。(157 Words)

Words and Phrases	新出単語・表現の意味を調べよう		
superconducting 形 [sùːpərkəndʌ́ktɪŋ]	1.	linear 形 [líniər]	2.
electromagnet 名 [ɪlèktroumǽgnɪt]	3.	magnet 名 [mǽgnɪt]	4.
ensure 動 [ɪnʃʊ́ər] B1	5.	gap 名 [gǽp] B1	6.
rail 名 [réɪl] B1	7.	friction 名 [fríkʃ(ə)n]	8.
current 形 [kə́ːr(ə)nt] B1	9.	construction 名 [kənstrʌ́kʃ(ə)n] B1	10.
be under construction	11.	throughout 前 [θruáʊt] B1	12.

A 【Comprehension 1】 Fill in the blanks in Japanese.

要点を整理しよう【思考力・判断力・表現力】

リニア新幹線

仕組み	(1.　　　　　　　) によって生み出される力を推進力とする →レールと車輪の (2.　　　　　　　) による速度の損失が起こらない
利点	現在の新幹線よりもずっと高速ではるかに (3.　　　　　　　) が少ない

高速鉄道の展望

鉄道はガソリン車や飛行機と比べて
(4.　　　　　　　) によい
↓
高速鉄道が世界の輸送において重要な役割を果たすだろう

B 【Comprehension 2】 Answer the following questions in English.

本文のポイントについて答えよう【思考力・判断力・表現力】

1. Why can the maglev train avoid any loss of speed?

2. What are the two advantages of the maglev train over the current train?

3. How is people's awareness changing now?

C 【Key Sentences】 Fill in the blanks and translate the following sentences.

重要文について確認しよう【知識・技能】【思考力・判断力・表現力】

④ **Not touching the rails**, the train avoids any loss of speed caused by friction between the rails and the wheels.

◆ not を用いた分詞構文の否定形は「理由」を表している。

訳：

⑤ **This system** will **allow** the train **to run** much faster and to cause far less noise than the current bullet train.

◆ this system＝(1.　　　　　[日本語で]) によって生み出される力の推進力を利用したシステム。
◆ allow＋O＋to 〜「O が〜できるようにする」。

訳：

⑫ The day will soon arrive **when** high-speed railways will **play a leading role in** transportation throughout the world.

◆関係副詞 when を含む節の先行詞は (2.　　　　　[英語2語で])。
◆ play a leading role in ... は「…で (3.　　　　　[日本語で]) を果たす」の意味。

訳：

Activity Plus 教科書p.26 ◁意味のまとまりに注意して，本文全体を聞こう。 ◉1-24

①After learning / about the development of high-speed railways, / a student wrote a short essay / about one of his memories / of railway travel / in an English class. //

②When I was younger, / my father often took my family / on several-day trips. // ③I remember visiting Mt. Aso, / Himeji Castle, / the Japan Alps, / and other places. // ④All these trips were great fun, / but there was one thing / I didn't like so much. // ⑤Many times, / though not always, / we made a trip / by car. // ⑥My father drove his car / all the way / during the trip, / because he really likes driving. // ⑦Traveling by car / was convenient and inexpensive / for my family, / to be sure, / but going along an expressway / for many hours / made me bored and sleepy. //

⑧I remember making a family trip / to Noto Peninsula / by train / when I was twelve years old. // ⑨We took a limited express train / to Kanazawa, / where we changed to a local train / that ran much slower / and stopped at every station. // ⑩It took us / a long time / to reach the station / where we got off, / but I had a very good time / on the train. // ⑪Looking out of the window of the train, / I enjoyed the scenery / of mountains, sea, coastline and local towns / that we couldn't have seen / from a car on an expressway. //

⑫I think slower trains enable us / to enjoy travel / in a more relaxed way. // ⑬Faster trains, / such as the Shinkansen, / are very convenient / for business trips and commuting long distances, / but in my free time / I would like to travel by slower trains / when possible. //

◁意味のまとまりに注意して，本文全体を音読しよう。（184 Words）

Words and Phrases 新出単語・表現の意味を調べよう			
essay 名[éseɪ] A2	1.	Alps 名[ǽlps]	2.
all the way	3.	inexpensive 形 [ìnɪkspénsɪv] A2	4.
to be sure	5.	expressway 名 [ɪkspréswèɪ]	6.
peninsula 名[pəníns(ə)lə]	7.	get off	8.
coastline 名[kóʊstlàɪn] B2	9.		

A【Comprehension 1】Fill in the blanks in Japanese.

要点を整理しよう【思考力・判断力・表現力】

子供のころに 行った家族旅行	自動車での旅行 が多かった ・長所：便利で（1.　　　　　　　）があまりかからない ・短所：高速道路の移動は（2.　　　　　　　）で眠くなる
鉄道旅行の 思い出	家族旅行にて能登半島で（3.　　　　　　　）に乗った ・車窓からの（4.　　　　　　）を楽しんだ
鉄道旅行に 関する意見	・鈍行列車はくつろぎながら旅行を楽しむことができる ・高速鉄道は（5.　　　　　　）や（6.　　　　　　　）を通勤するときは便利 だ →可能なときは（7.　　　　　　）で旅行をしたい

B【Comprehension 2】Answer the following questions in English.

本文のポイントについて答えよう【思考力・判断力・表現力】

1.　How did the student's family make a trip many times?

2.　What did the student's family take to travel from Kanazawa?

3.　In the student's opinion, what can we do if we take a slower train?

C【Key Sentences】Fill in the blanks and translate the following sentences.

重要文について確認しよう【知識・技能】【思考力・判断力・表現力】

⑦　Traveling by car was convenient and inexpensive for my family, to be sure, but going along an expressway for many hours made me bored and sleepy.
　　◆文の構造を見極めることが大切。この文の動詞は（1.　　　[英語1語で]）と（2.　　　[英語1語で]）。
　　訳 :

⑨　We took a limited express train to <u>Kanazawa</u>, **where** we changed to a local train **that** ran much slower and stopped at every station.
　　◆関係副詞 where の非制限用法。「そこで」というように補足的に説明するように訳すとよい。
　　◆ that は関係代名詞。先行詞（3.　　　　　　[英語3語で]）を修飾している。
　　訳 :

⑫　I think slower trains **enable** us **to enjoy** travel in a more relaxed way.
　　◆ enable＋O＋to ～「O が～することを可能にする」。
　　訳 :

Paragraphs 1～3

教科書 p.32 🔊意味のまとまりに注意して，本文全体を聞こう。 🎧1-26

①Many of us take safe drinking water for granted, / even though more than 600 million people / worldwide / must depend on / unclean water every day. //

[1] ②In many parts of Africa / and some Southeast Asian countries, / there is no tap water. // ③In many cases, / women and children have to use / river water / for their everyday needs. // ④It takes them hours / to carry it home. // ⑤They may be attacked / by dangerous wild animals / on their way. // ⑥The task of carrying water / every day / is so tough / that many children cannot go to school. //

[2] ⑦What is worse, / the water people depend on / is often muddy or unclean. // ⑧Even after they safely return home, / the polluted water sometimes causes fatal diseases / like cholera. // ⑨Some families have their own wells, / but / unless the wells are deep enough, / the water in them / may be contaminated. //

[3] ⑩The need for water / can trigger conflicts / between groups of people. // ⑪In Kenya, / two tribes were on the verge of fighting / each other / over the water / from a river. // ⑫A farming tribe / living in a village upstream / made a dam / for their crops, / and the herding tribe / living downstream / got so angry / that they armed themselves / in preparation for retaking the water. // ⑬Fortunately, / the police intervened / in the dispute, / and fighting was narrowly avoided. //

🔊意味のまとまりに注意して，本文全体を音読しよう。（188 Words）

Words and Phrases 新出単語・表現の意味を調べよう			
take ... for granted	1.	grant 動[grǽnt] B1	2.
southeast 形[sàʊθíːst] B1	3.	what is worse	4.
muddy 形[mʌ́di] B2	5.	fatal 形[féɪt(ə)l] B2	6.
cholera 名[kɑ́(:)l(ə)rə]	7.	contaminate 動[kəntǽmɪnèɪt] B2	8.
trigger 動[trígər]	9.	conflict 名[kɑ́(:)nflɪkt] B1	10.
tribe 名[tráɪb] B2	11.	verge 名[vɚːdʒ]	12.

on the verge of ...	13.	upstream 副 [ʌ̀pstríːm]	14.
herd 動 [hə́ːrd]	15.	downstream 副 [dàunstríːm]	16.
in preparation for ...	17.	retake 動 [rìːtéɪk]	18.
intervene 動 [ìntərvíːn]	19.	dispute 名 [dɪspjúːt] B2	20.
narrowly 副 [nǽrouli] B2	21.		

A 【Comprehension 1】 Fill in the blanks in Japanese.

要点を整理しよう【思考力・判断力・表現力】

世界各地（アフリカ・東南アジア）の水問題

背景	(1.　　　　　　　) がない　→　日常生活に川の水を使用
問題	・川の水を家まで運ぶのに何時間もかかる 　→危険な（2.　　　　　　　）に襲われる／子供が（3.　　　　　　　）に行けなくなる ・汚染された水が致命的な病気を引き起こす 　→深い（4.　　　　　　　）でなければ，水が汚染されている可能性がある
具体例	ケニアで２つの民族が川の水をめぐって（5.　　　　　　　）の危機に至った

B 【Comprehension 2】 Answer the following questions in English.

本文のポイントについて答えよう【思考力・判断力・表現力】

1. What water do women and children have to use for their everyday needs?

2. What issues are there concerning the wells some families own?

C 【Key Sentence】 Translate the following sentence.

重要文について確認しよう【知識・技能】【思考力・判断力・表現力】

⑫ A farming tribe (living in a village upstream) made a dam for their crops, and the herding tribe (living downstream) got **so** angry **that** they armed themselves in preparation for retaking the water.

◆現在分詞 living は，それぞれ直前の名詞 a farming tribe，the herding tribe を修飾している。
◆〈so＋形容詞＋that ～〉は「とても…なので～」という意味。

訳：

25

Paragraphs 4～6

教科書 p.33　◁意味のまとまりに注意して，本文全体を聞こう。1-28

4 ①Atsushi Ono, / who used to work / as a construction site supervisor, / found an article / published by an NGO. // ②It was about digging wells / for clean water / in Zambia / with the traditional Japanese method / called *Kazusabori*. // ③This article reminded him / of his grandfather, / who was a well-driller, / and he became interested / in the project. //

5 ④*Kazusabori* was developed / in the Kazusa area / in Chiba Prefecture. // ⑤Drillers can dig / into the ground / as deep as several hundred meters / until fresh underground water comes out. // ⑥This method only requires human power / and building materials / that are available locally. // ⑦Although its use declined / in Japan / after the machine-drilling system was developed, / this method has been welcomed / in developing countries. //

6 ⑧Ono applied / to join the project and, / thanks to his experience / in construction, / he was chosen / as a member. // ⑨After training / in digging wells / and speaking English, / he went to Meheba, / a town / in the northern part of Zambia, / where there were many refugees / from neighboring countries. // ⑩Ono's team began digging, / and when the depth of the well reached / about 25 meters, / water came out. // ⑪That was the moment / when his first well was successful. //

◁意味のまとまりに注意して，本文全体を音読しよう。（189 Words）

Words and Phrases 新出単語・表現の意味を調べよう			
supervisor 名 [súːpərvàɪzər] B2	1.	Zambia [zǽmbiə]	2.
remind 動 [rɪmáɪnd] A2	3.	remind A of B	4.
driller 名 [drílər]	5.	underground 形 [ʌ́ndərgràʊnd] B2	6.
come out	7.	Meheba [məhébə]	メヘバ
depth 名 [dépθ] B1	8.		

A 【Comprehension 1】 Fill in the blanks in Japanese.

要点を整理しよう【思考力・判断力・表現力】

大野さんが井戸を完成させるまでのいきさつ

ザンビアで井戸を掘るプロジェクトについての (1.　　　　　　　)を見つける	➡	プロジェクトに (2.　　　　　　)して，メンバーに選ばれる	➡	メヘバという町に行き，井戸掘りをおこない，水を掘り当てる

上総掘り：千葉県の上総地方で開発された伝統的な技術。数（3.　　）メートルの掘削が可能。

必要なもの 人の力と（4.　　　　　　）で手に入る建材。

B 【Comprehension 2】 Answer the following questions in English.

本文のポイントについて答えよう【思考力・判断力・表現力】

1. What was the article about that Ono was interested in?

2. What can drillers do with the method of *Kazusabori*?

3. What did Ono do before going to a town in Zambia?

C 【Key Sentences】 Fill in the blanks and translate the following sentences.

重要文について確認しよう【知識・技能】【思考力・判断力・表現力】

③ This article **reminded** him **of** his grandfather, (**who** was a well-driller,) **and** he became interested in the project.

◆ remind A of B は「A に B を（1.　　　　　　[日本語で]）」という意味。
◆関係代名詞は非制限用法。and は 2 つの文を結んでいる。
訳：

⑦ Although **its use** declined in Japan after the machine-drilling system was developed, this method **has been welcomed** in developing countries.

◆ its use＝(2.　　　　　[日本語で]) を利用すること
◆〈have＋been＋過去分詞〉は現在完了形の受動態で，ここでは継続の意味。
訳：

⑨ After training in digging wells and speaking English, he went to Meheba, 〈a town in the northern part of Zambia,〉 (**where** there were many refugees from neighboring countries).

◆ Meheba は挿入句で同格的に説明され，さらに関係副詞の先行詞となっている。
訳：

Paragraphs 7〜9

教科書 p.34　🔊意味のまとまりに注意して，本文全体を聞こう。　◎1-30

7　①During his work, / Ono trained the local people / so that they could continue / to dig wells / on their own. // ②He taught them / to replace the materials / used in traditional *Kazusabori* / with more suitable ones / for Africa. // ③He also changed some technical Japanese terms / into plain English words. // ④There is a saying / he cherishes: / "If your friends are hungry, / do not give them / fish, / but teach them / how to catch / them." // ⑤He thinks / that teaching well-digging techniques / to local people / is better than simply making wells / for them. //

8　⑥Ono later established an NPO, / the International Water Project (IWP). // ⑦Although there have been many hardships / in its operation, / it has completed / more than 100 wells / so far. // ⑧Besides digging wells, / the members are teaching children / the importance of planting and growing trees / for the future. //

9　⑨A supply of clean water ensures improved health, / good education, / and work opportunities. // ⑩Universal and equitable access / to safe and affordable drinking water / is one of the SDG targets / which we need to achieve / by 2030. // ⑪The traditional Japanese *Kazusabori* method / is playing an important role / in achieving this target. //

🔊意味のまとまりに注意して，本文全体を音読しよう。（183 Words）

Words　新出単語の意味を調べよう			
suitable 形 [súːtəb(ə)l] A2	1.	technical 形 [téknɪk(ə)l] B2	2.
cherish 動 [tʃérɪʃ] B1	3.	universal 形 [jùːnɪvə́ːrs(ə)l] B2	4.
equitable 形 [ékwətəb(ə)l] B1	5.	access 名 [ǽksəs] B1	6.
affordable 形 [əfɔ́ːrdəb(ə)l] B2	7.		

A 【**Comprehension 1**】 Fill in the blanks in Japanese.

要点を整理しよう【思考力・判断力・表現力】

大野さんの考え方と NPO の活動

| 現地の人たちに井戸を掘る技術を (1.　　　　) こと　＞ | 彼らのために井戸を (2.　　　) こと |
| よりよいこと |

NPO（インターナショナル・ウォーター・プロジェクト）の設立
・これまでに100本以上の［100本を超える］井戸を完成
・(3.　　　) を植え，育てることの大切さを子供たちに伝える

安全で安価な飲料水を普遍的かつ衡平に入手できること：(4.　　　　　　) のターゲットのひとつ

B 【**Comprehension 2**】 Answer the following questions in English.

本文のポイントについて答えよう【思考力・判断力・表現力】

1. What did Ono do to make it easier for the local people to understand better?

2. What has the NPO that Ono established completed so far?

3. What does a supply of clean water ensure?

C 【**Key Sentences**】 Fill in the blanks and translate the following sentences.

重要文について確認しよう【知識・技能】【思考力・判断力・表現力】

① During his work, Ono trained the local people **so that** they **could** continue to dig wells **on their own**.

◆ so that … could ～で「…が～できる［できた］ように」という目的を表す。
◆ on one's own は (1.　　　　[日本語で]) という意味。
訳 :

⑦ Although **there have been** many hardships in its operation, **it** has completed more than 100 wells so far.

◆ there have been … は，there is 構文を現在完了形で表したもの。
◆ it ＝ (2.　　　　　　　　　　　　[英語4語で])
訳 :

⑩ Universal and equitable access (to safe and affordable drinking water) is one of
                                                                            S   V   C

   the SDG targets (**which** we need to achieve by 2030).

◆ to で始まる形容詞句が直前の universal and equitable access を修飾している。
◆ which で始まる関係代名詞節が直前の one of the SDG targets を修飾している。SDG は「SDGs に関する」の意味の形容詞で，形容詞では -s を付けずに用いる。
訳 :

Activity Plus 教科書 p.38 ◀意味のまとまりに注意して，本文全体を聞こう。 ◎1-32

①You are looking / at a crowdfunding website / and discussing / which group you will donate to. //

②Water for Cambodia // ③Reward: / Local farm products / like raw sugar // ④Be the first to donate / $0 of $5,000 // ⑤Cambodia is a nation rich in water. // ⑥The water in many areas / is clean / and drinkable. // ⑦Nevertheless, / the ground / in some areas of Cambodia / contains chemicals / poisonous to humans. // ⑧In such areas, / underground water needs to be filtered / with special kinds of plastic fiber. // ⑨We have been working / for decades / with a Japanese company / which has technology / for filtering water / and have been assisting farmers / in Cambodia. //

⑩Water for Myanmar // ⑪Reward: / A piece of handicraft // ⑫Last donation: / 7 hours ago / $3,700 of $7,500 // ⑬Sea water is available / to many people / in areas / along sea coasts, / especially in the refugee camps / along the coasts of Myanmar / and Bangladesh. // ⑭When sea water is filtered / with a special fiber, / it becomes fresh water. // ⑮Unfortunately, / it often costs / more than 1 US dollar / to make 1 cubic meter of fresh water. // ⑯With 3 US dollars / a day, / we can provide fresh water / to save the lives / of more than 2 refugees. // ⑰Your pocket money will save lives! //

⑱Assistance for India // ⑲Reward: / A package of Indian tea / (for a donation of 20 US dollars or more) // ⑳Last donation: / 15 minutes ago / $5,900 of $6,000 // ㉑When it comes to filtering, / it costs less / to turn waste water into clean water / than it does / to turn sea water into fresh water. // ㉒The processed water can be used / for farming and toilets, / and it also reduces / the large amount of waste water / flowing into rivers. // ㉓In India, where waste from toilets is a serious issue, / this project will solve / not only water shortages, / but also sewage problems. // ㉔We appreciate your help / in improving public hygiene / in India. //

㉕The Ugandan Well Foundation // ㉖Reward: / Your name will be carved into a well // ㉗Last donation: / 7 hours ago / $15,000 of $10,000 // ㉘The Ugandan Well Foundation, / together with local partners, / provides access / to clean water. // ㉙Unfortunately, / we lack money / and cannot purchase enough machines and materials / to drill wells. // ㉚Some of the existing wells are old and need repairing, / but the local people don't know / how to fix them. // ㉛We are waiting for your donation. // ㉜It costs $2,000 / to build a new well, / and $500 / to fix an old one. //

◀意味のまとまりに注意して，本文全体を音読しよう。（373 Words）

Words and Phrases 新出単語・表現の意味を調べよう			
crowdfunding 名 [kráʊdfÀndɪŋ]	1.	Cambodia [kæmbóʊdiə]	2.

reward 名[rɪwɔ́ːrd] B1	3.	raw 形[rɔ́ː] A2	4.
drinkable 形 [dríŋkəb(ə)l] B2	5.	poisonous 形 [pɔ́ɪz(ə)nəs] B1	6.
filter 動[fíltər]	7.	fiber 名[fáɪbər] B2	8.
Myanmar [míːənmɑːr]	9.	handicraft 名 [hǽndikræft] B2	10.
coast 名[kóʊst] A2	11.	Bangladesh [bæ̀ŋglədéʃ]	12.
cubic 形[kjúːbɪk]	13.	flow 動[flóʊ] B1	14.
sewage 名[súːɪdʒ]	15.	hygiene 名[háɪdʒiːn] B2	16.
Ugandan 形[juɡǽndən]	17.	carve 動[kɑ́ːrv] B2	18.
together with …	19.		

A 【Comprehension 1】 Fill in the blanks in Japanese.

要点を整理しよう【思考力・判断力・表現力】

Water for Cambodia	Water for Myanmar
現地の課題：有害な（1. 　　　　　）を含んだ地面がある。 **取り組み内容**：（2. 　　　　　）の企業と協力し，地下水をろ過して農家を支援している。	**取り組み内容**：（3. 　　　　　）をろ過して真水にすることで，沿岸に住む（4. 　　　　　）を支援している。 **取り組みの課題**：多くの費用がかかる。
Assistance for India	The Ugandan Well Foundation
現地の課題：大量の廃棄物が（5. 　　　　　）に流されている。 **取り組み内容**：排水をろ過して農業用水や（6. 　　　　　）の水に使えるようにする。	**取り組み内容**：井戸を掘って清潔な水が入手できる手段を提供している。 **取り組みの課題**：資金が不足しており，機械や資材を十分に（7. 　　　　　）できない。

B 【Comprehension 2】 Answer the following questions in English.

本文のポイントについて答えよう【思考力・判断力・表現力】

1. Why does some underground water in Cambodia need to be filtered?

----

2. Which of the four groups would be the best option to help people who have been forced to leave their countries?

Paragraphs 1～3

教科書 p.44 🔊意味のまとまりに注意して，本文全体を聞こう。 ◉1-34

①What messages can we get / from athletes / in order to make our society / more sensitive / to human rights? //

1　②"Well, / what was the message / that you got? // ③That was more the question. // ④The point is / to make people start talking," / said professional tennis player / Naomi Osaka / when the interviewer asked her / what message she wanted to send / to the spectators. //

2　⑤Born to a Haitian father / and a Japanese mother, / Naomi has become / a prominent tennis player. // ⑥In the 2020 U.S. Open Championships, / she won seven matches / and got her third grand-slam trophy. // ⑦In each game, / she appeared / with a mask / which had the name / of a different African-American / who had been killed / by white civilians / or police officers / for no good reason. // ⑧Her "message" was symbolized / in the names / on the seven masks / she wore. // ⑨She said, / "Before I am an athlete, / I am a black woman." //

3　⑩Another Japanese athlete / who shares a racial background / similar to Naomi's / is Rui Hachimura, / the NBA star. // ⑪He was born in Toyama City / to a Japanese mother / and a Beninese father, / so he stood out / in his neighborhood / because of his skin color. // ⑫"People looked at me / as if to say, / 'You are different.' // ⑬I was always trying / to hide from them," / he recalls. //

🔊意味のまとまりに注意して，本文全体を音読しよう。（192 Words）

Words and Phrases 新出単語・表現の意味を調べよう			
sensitive 形 [sénsətɪv] B2	1.	be sensitive to …	2.
Haitian 形 [héɪʃ(ə)n]	3.	prominent 形 [prɑ́(:)mɪnənt] B1	4.
trophy 名 [tróufi] B2	5.	civilian 名 [səvíliən]	6.
symbolize 動 [símbəlàɪz]	7.	racial 形 [réɪʃ(ə)l] B1	8.
background 名 [bǽkgràʊnd] A2	9.	be similar to …	10.
Beninese 形 [bènɪníːz]	11.	stand out	12.
as if to say …	13.		

A 【Comprehension 1】 Fill in the blanks in Japanese.

要点を整理しよう【思考力・判断力・表現力】

	大坂なおみ選手	八村塁選手
競技	(1.　　　　　　　)	バスケットボール（NBA）
生まれ	父親：(2.　　　　　　) 人 母親：日本人	父親：ベナン人 母親：(3.　　　　　) 人
エピソード	2020年の全米オープンで，アフリカ系アメリカ人の名前が書かれた (4.　　　　　　) を着けて登場した。	生まれ故郷では，近所で（5.　　　　　　）の色が目立っていたので，近所の人から隠れようとしていた。

B 【Comprehension 2】 Answer the following questions in English.

本文のポイントについて答えよう【思考力・判断力・表現力】

1. What did Naomi Osaka want people to do?

　　　　　　　　　　　　　　　　　　　　　　　　　　　　　

2. What had happened to the African-Americans whose names were on Naomi's masks?

　　　　　　　　　　　　　　　　　　　　　　　　　　　　　

3. What was Rui Hachimura always trying to do when he was in his hometown?

　　　　　　　　　　　　　　　　　　　　　　　　　　　　　

C 【Key Sentences】 Fill in the blank and translate the following sentences.

重要文について確認しよう【知識・技能】【思考力・判断力・表現力】

⑤ **Born** to a Haitian father and a Japanese mother, Naomi has become a prominent tennis player.

◆過去分詞 born で始まる分詞構文で，付帯状況を表す。born to ... で「…の子として生まれて」という意味。意味上の主語は（1.　　　　[英語1語で]）。

訳：　　　　　　　　　　　　　　　　　　　　　　　　　　

⑦ In each game, she appeared with a mask (**which** had the name of a different African-American (**who** had been killed by white civilians or police officers **for no good reason**)).

◆ which と who はどちらも関係代名詞。それぞれ直前の名詞を修飾している。

◆述語動詞 appeared は過去形。その時点より前であることを示すために had been killed は過去完了。

◆ for no good reason は「正当な理由もなく」の意味。

訳：

Paragraphs 4～6

教科書 p.45 ◀意味のまとまりに注意して，本文全体を聞こう。 1-36

④ ①Rui was born a natural athlete. // ②He was very good at all sorts of sports, / and people around him began / to respect him. // ③He started playing basketball / in junior high school, / and eventually / he became an NBA player. // ④Rui said, / "I started / to think it's good / to be who I am. // ⑤I'm unique. // ⑥I'm always proud / of myself." // ⑦He supported the movement / against racial discrimination / together / with his teammates / by kneeling / during the national anthem / before games. //

⑤ ⑧The world of sports / has had a strong relationship / with social issues / for a long time. // ⑨However, / while many biracial athletes have given great performances / in Japan, / it has been very rare / that these athletes, / let alone other non-biracial Japanese athletes, / have raised their voices / about human rights. // ⑩Japanese athletes particularly / "tend to think / it is a virtue / to focus only on their own competitions, / not on social issues. // ⑪It's a pity," / says Dai Tamesue, / an Olympian. //

⑥ ⑫It is not only in Japan / that athletics and social issues / have been kept separate. // ⑬The International Olympic Committee (IOC) / has long tried / to separate itself / from politics / in society. //

◀意味のまとまりに注意して，本文全体を音読しよう。（184 Words）

Words and Phrases	新出単語・表現の意味を調べよう		
discrimination 名 [dɪskrɪ̀mɪnéɪʃ(ə)n] B1	1.	kneel 動 [ní:l] B2	2.
anthem 名 [ǽnθəm]	3.	relationship 名 [rɪléɪʃ(ə)nʃɪp] B1	4.
biracial 形 [baɪréɪʃ(ə)l]	5.	let alone	6.
virtue 名 [vɜ́:rtʃu:] B2	7.	raise one's voice	8.
Olympian 名 [əlímpiən]	9.	committee 名 [kəmíti] A2	10.
separate A from B	11.	politics 名 [pá(:)lətìks] B1	12.

A 【Comprehension 1】 Fill in the blanks in Japanese.

要点を整理しよう【思考力・判断力・表現力】

八村選手の行動	NBA の試合前の国歌斉唱中に（1. ） →（2. ）に反対する運動の支援
日本の状況	アスリートが（3. ）について声をあげることはまれ →日本人アスリートは「社会問題ではなく（4. ）だけに集中することが美徳だと考える傾向がある」（為末大氏：元オリンピック選手）
世界の状況	国際オリンピック委員会は長い間，（5. ）から距離を置こうとしてきた

B 【Comprehension 2】 Answer the following questions in English.

本文のポイントについて答えよう【思考力・判断力・表現力】

1. How did Rui and his teammates support the movement against racial discrimination?

2. According to Dai Tamesue, what do Japanese athletes tend to think is a virtue?

3. What has the International Olympic Committee tried to do?

C 【Key Sentences】 Fill in the blank and translate the following sentences.

重要文について確認しよう【知識・技能】【思考力・判断力・表現力】

④ I started to think **it**'s good to be who I am.
◆ it は形式主語。真主語は to-不定詞以下。
◆ who I am は「（1. ）」という意味。
訳：

⑨ However, **while** many biracial athletes have given great performances in Japan, it has been very rare that these athletes, ⟨**let alone** other non-biracial Japanese athletes,⟩ have raised their voices about human rights.
◆接続詞 while は「…なのに対して」と，対比や譲歩を表すディスコースマーカー。主節は it has been … の節。
◆ let alone … はここでは挿入句として使われている。
訳：

⑫ **It is** not only in Japan **that** athletics and social issues have been kept separate.
◆ It is 〜 that … の形は強調構文。not only in Japan の部分が強調されている。
◆この separate は形容詞で「別々の」という意味。S＋V＋O＋C の O が受動態で前に出ている。
訳：

Paragraphs 7～9

教科書 p.46 ◀意味のまとまりに注意して，本文全体を聞こう。 ◎1-38

7 ①The history of the Olympics reminds us / of a well-known protest. // ②At the awards ceremony / for the 1968 Olympic Games / in Mexico City, / the first- and third-place winners / of the men's 200-meter track event, / both of whom were African-Americans / from the U.S., / looked down / and raised their fists / in black gloves / while the national anthem was being played. // ③This action was a protest / against the racial discrimination / in American society / at that time. // ④Such acts were strictly prohibited / by the Olympic Charter. // ⑤As a result, / they were sent back / to their country. //

8 ⑥The messages from athletes / have strong impacts / on society. // ⑦Their athletic performances and voices can encourage us / to become aware / of and more sensitive / to social issues. // ⑧As Rui says, / their performances can "inspire not only young players / in Japan / but also kids of mixed race / struggling with racism, / discrimination and identity issues." //

9 ⑨Racial discrimination can occur anywhere. // ⑩It is not limited / to the U.S., / and it should be considered / a clear violation / of human rights. // ⑪What is the message / you've gotten? // ⑫Athletes' actions send us messages, / just like Naomi wanted to send hers / to us. //

◀意味のまとまりに注意して，本文全体を音読しよう。（188 Words）

Words and Phrases 新出単語・表現の意味を調べよう			
Mexico City [méksɪkòusíti]	メキシコシティ	fist 图 [físt]	1.
glove 图 [glʌ́v] A2	2.	strictly 副 [strík(t)li] B2	3.
charter 图 [tʃɑ́ːrtər]	4.	struggle with …	5.
racism 图 [réɪsɪz(ə)m] B2	6.	be limited to …	7.
violation 图 [vàɪəléɪʃ(ə)n]	8.		

A 【Comprehension 1】 Fill in the blanks in Japanese.

要点を整理しよう【思考力・判断力・表現力】

◆アスリートによる抗議行動の事例

いつ	1968年のメキシコシティオリンピックの（1.　　　　　）式
だれが	米国出身の2人のアフリカ系アメリカ人選手
何をしたか	国歌の演奏中，下を向きながら黒い手袋をした（2.　　　　　）を挙げて，（3.　　　　　）に対する抗議を示した
その結果	（4.　　　　　）に抵触する行為だったため本国に送還された

◆アスリートがメッセージを発することの意味
・人々が（5.　　　　　）に気づき，より敏感になる
◆人種差別とは
・どこでも起こり得る問題であり，明らかな（6.　　　　　）である

B 【Comprehension 2】 Answer the following questions in English.

本文のポイントについて答えよう【思考力・判断力・表現力】

1. Looking down and raising their fists in black gloves, what were the African-American athletes from the U.S. against?

2. What can the athletic performances and voices encourage us to do?

3. Where can racial discrimination occur?

C 【Key Sentences】 Translate the following sentences.

重要文について確認しよう【知識・技能】【思考力・判断力・表現力】

② … the first- and third-place winners of the men's 200-meter track event, (**both of whom** were African-Americans from the U.S.,) looked down and raised their fists in black gloves while the national anthem **was being played**.
◆both of whom … は，「その両方が…」というように先行詞を補足的に説明している。
◆〈be-動詞＋being＋過去分詞〉は進行形の受動態で，「〜されているところだ」の意味。
訳：

⑧ **As** Rui says, their performances can "inspire not only young players in Japan but also kids of mixed race (**struggling** with racism, discrimination and identity issues)."
◆as は様態を表す。「(八村)塁選手が言うように」。
◆not only A but also B の B で，現在分詞 struggling が直前の名詞句を修飾している。
訳：

Activity Plus 教科書 p.50 ◁意味のまとまりに注意して，本文全体を聞こう。 ◎1-40

①You are learning / about the relationship / between the Olympics and human rights. // ②You found an article / about Rule 50 of the Olympic Charter. //

③50: / Advertising, / demonstrations, / propaganda //

④"No kind of demonstration / or political, / religious / or racial propaganda / is permitted / in any Olympic sites, / venues or other areas." //

⑤Why does this rule exist / and what does it aim / to achieve? //

⑥The focus at the Olympic Games / must remain on athletes' performances, / sport / and the international unity / and harmony / that the Olympic Movement seeks / to advance. // ⑦Athletes at the Olympic Games / are part of a global community / with many different views, / lifestyles / and values. // ⑧The mission of the Olympic Games / to bring the entire world together / can facilitate the understanding / of different views, / but this can be accomplished / only if everybody respects / this diversity. //

⑨Where are protests and demonstrations not permitted? //

⑩At all Olympic venues, / including: / On the field of play // ⑪In the Olympic village // ⑫During Olympic medal ceremonies // ⑬During the opening, / closing / and other official ceremonies //

⑭Any protest or demonstration / outside Olympic venues / must comply with local legislation / wherever local law forbids such actions. //

⑮Where do athletes have the opportunity / to express their views? //

⑯While respecting local laws, / athletes have the opportunity / to express their opinions, / including: / During interviews // ⑰At team meetings // ⑱On digital / or traditional media //

⑲It should be noted / that expressing views / is different / from protesting and demonstrating. //

⑳Here are some examples / of what would constitute a protest, / as opposed to expressing views: // ㉑Displaying any political messages // ㉒Gestures of a political nature / (Kneeling is permitted / before games.) // ㉓Refusal to follow the ceremonies protocol //   ◁意味のまとまりに注意して，本文全体を音読しよう。(242 Words)

Words and Phrases 新出単語・表現の意味を調べよう			
advertising 名 [ǽdvərtàɪzɪŋ] A2	1.	demonstration 名 [dèmənstréɪʃ(ə)n] B1	2.

propaganda 名 [prà(:)pəgǽndə]	3.	religious 形 [rɪlídʒəs] B1	4.
venue 名 [vénjuː] B2	5.	bring … together	6.
unity 名 [júːnəti]	7.	seek 動 [síːk] A2	8.
value 名 [vǽljuː] A2	9.	mission 名 [míʃ(ə)n] B1	10.
facilitate 動 [fəsílətèit] B2	11.	diversity 名 [dəvə́ːrsəti]	12.
comply 動 [kəmplái]	13.	legislation 名 [lèdʒɪsléɪʃ(ə)n] B2	14.
forbid 動 [fərbíd] A2	15.	constitute 動 [kɑ́(:)nstətjùːt] B1	16.
oppose 動 [əpóuz] A2	17.	as opposed to …	18.
gesture 名 [dʒéstʃər] B1	19.	refusal 名 [rɪfjúːz(ə)l] B1	20.
protocol 名 [próutəkà(:)l]	21.		

A 【Comprehension 1】 Fill in the blanks in Japanese.

要点を整理しよう【思考力・判断力・表現力】

オリンピック憲章第50条（広告，デモ，プロパガンダの禁止）

規則の存在意義と目的：オリンピックの焦点は，アスリートの演技，スポーツ競技，国際的な結束と（1.　　　　　　）にある。オリンピックの使命は異なる見解の理解を促進するが，これはすべての人が（2.　　　　　　）を尊重した場合においてのみ達成される。	
許可事項	（3.　　　　　）事項
以下の場面における自分の意見表明 （4.　　　　　　）／チームミーティング／デジタルメディアや紙媒体メディア	以下の場所での抗議行動やデモ 競技場／選手村／メダル授与式／開会式，閉会式，その他の公式セレモニー

B 【Comprehension 2】 Answer the following questions in English.

本文のポイントについて答えよう【思考力・判断力・表現力】

1. In what condition can the mission of the Olympic Games be accomplished?

----

2. What is required for protests or demonstrations outside Olympic venues?

Paragraphs 1~3

教科書 p.56　🔊意味のまとまりに注意して，本文全体を聞こう。　⊚1-42

①Babies are often described / as "linguistic geniuses," / but we do not fully understand / the process of their language acquisition / or the challenges / they face. // ②Can you get any hints / for your learning / of English? //

1 ③Do you remember / how you learned / your first language? // ④Probably none of you do. // ⑤Even so, / you may think / that babies master their first language, / or mother tongue, / with little difficulty. // ⑥Is that true? // ⑦Research findings from infant studies / suggest that babies, / despite their talent, / need much time and effort / to master language. //

2 ⑧Language acquisition begins / when babies start / to perceive sounds. // ⑨More precisely, / they first need / to become aware / that people around them use language / to communicate with each other. // ⑩Babies are then required / to identify words / (e.g., / "milk") / from a series of unfamiliar sounds / (e.g., / do you want / some milk?) / to understand / what people are saying. // ⑪It may be surprising / to know / that most babies seem / to develop this ability / by the age of eight months. //

3 ⑫Babies do not learn language / by themselves; / assistance from people / around them / is essential / for their language development. // ⑬For example, / caregivers often use a clearer, simplified form / of speech / called "baby talk" / to interact with small children. // ⑭A large-scale study / conducted across cultures and continents / has shown that babies respond better / to baby talk / than to normal adult speech. //

🔊意味のまとまりに注意して，本文全体を音読しよう。（189 Words）

Words and Phrases 新出単語・表現の意味を調べよう			
linguistic 形 [lɪŋgwístɪk]	1.	genius 名 [dʒíːniəs] B2	2.
acquisition 名 [æ̀kwɪzíʃ(ə)n] B2	3.	infant 名 [ínf(ə)nt] B2	4.
despite 前 [dɪspáɪt] B1	5.	talent 名 [tǽlənt] A2	6.
perceive 動 [pərsíːv] B2	7.	precisely 副 [prɪsáɪsli] B2	8.
series 名 [síəriːz] B1	9.	a series of …	10.
unfamiliar 形 [ʌ̀nfəmíljər] B2	11.	caregiver 名 [kéəgɪvər]	12.

simplify 動 [símplɪfàɪ] B1	13.	large-scale 形 [làːrdʒskéɪl]	14.
conduct 動 [kəndʌ́kt] B2	15.		

A 【**Comprehension 1**】 Fill in the blanks in Japanese.

要点を整理しよう【思考力・判断力・表現力】

赤ちゃんが音声を理解する過程

・周りの人たちが言葉を使ってお互いに（1.　　　　　　）をとっていることを認識する。　➡　・一連の聞きなれない（2.　　　　　）から言葉を識別する。

生後（3.　　　　）か月までに発達

・言語能力の発達には周囲の人の援助が不可欠

例：明確で（4.　　　　）された話し方（＝ベビートーク）の使用

B 【**Comprehension 2**】 Answer the following questions in English.

本文のポイントについて答えよう【思考力・判断力・表現力】

1. When do babies develop their ability to identify words from a series of unfamiliar sounds?

　　--

2. According to a large-scale study, which is more effective in communicating with babies, baby talk or normal adult speech?

　　--

C 【**Key Sentences**】 Fill in the blank and translate the following sentences.

重要文について確認しよう【知識・技能】【思考力・判断力・表現力】

⑪ **It** may be surprising to know that most babies seem to develop **this ability** by the age of eight months.

◆ It は形式主語。真主語は to know 以下。

◆ this ability＝the ability to (1.　　　　　　　　　[英語 7 語で]） sounds

訳：--

⑭ A large-scale study (**conducted** across cultures and continents) has shown that babies respond better to baby talk │than│ to normal adult speech.

◆過去分詞 conducted は直前の A large-scale study を修飾している。

◆better A than B で「B より A のほうがよりよく」。A と B に前置詞 to の句がきている。

訳：--

　　--

41

Paragraphs 4〜6

教科書 p.57　🔊意味のまとまりに注意して，本文全体を聞こう。1-44

④ ①Just like with speech perception, / babies need / to pass through a number of stages / as they learn to talk. // ②From birth, / babies make a range of noises / such as crying and coughing. // ③They then start / to make cooing noises / like "ooh" and "aah." // ④By six to nine months, / they begin / to enjoy repeating certain sounds / such as "dada" and "gaga" / over and over / again. // ⑤This is commonly called "babbling." //

⑤ ⑥It is only after babies turn 12 months old / that they finally begin / to say a few simple words / such as "mama" and "mum." // ⑦Their vocabulary continues / to grow afterwards, / reaching about 200 words / in total / at around the age of 24 months. // ⑧Some babies are said / to experience a sudden growth / in their vocabulary / between 18 and 24 months of age. // ⑨This is called a "vocabulary spurt." //

⑥ ⑩Babies also learn to point at things / when they are between 12 and 18 months old. // ⑪Pointing is an essential tool / for their early communication / to show their desires / and draw attention, / especially when they cannot yet express themselves / well / in words. // ⑫After having elicited reactions / from others, / babies often begin to say a word / for something / that they have pointed to / previously. //

🔊意味のまとまりに注意して，本文全体を音読しよう。（200 Words）

Words and Phrases	新出単語・表現の意味を調べよう		
perception 名 [pərsépʃ(ə)n] B2	1.	from birth	2.
a range of …	3.	cough 動 [kɔ́:f] B1	4.
coo 動 [kú:]	5.	over and over again	6.
babble 動 [bǽb(ə)l]	7.	mama 名 [má:mə] B2	8.
vocabulary 名 [voukǽbjəlèri] A2	9.	afterwards 副 [ǽftərwərdz] B1	10.
spurt 名 [spə́:rt]	11.	point at …	12.
desire 名 [dɪzáɪər] B1	13.	draw attention	14.
elicit 動 [ɪlísət]	15.	reaction 名 [riǽkʃ(ə)n] B2	16.

A 【**Comprehension 1**】 Fill in the blanks in Japanese.

赤ちゃんの言語能力の発達過程

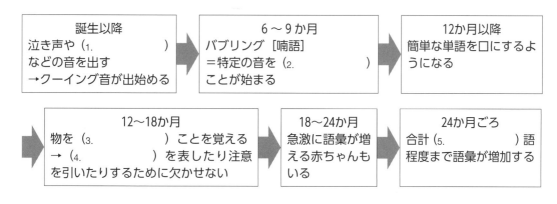

誕生以降 泣き声や（1.　　　　） などの音を出す →クーイング音が出始める	6〜9か月 バブリング［喃語］ ＝特定の音を（2.　　　　） ことが始まる	12か月以降 簡単な単語を口にするよ うになる
12〜18か月 物を（3.　　　　）ことを覚える →（4.　　　　）を表したり注意 を引いたりするために欠かせない	18〜24か月 急激に語彙が増 える赤ちゃんも いる	24か月ごろ 合計（5.　　　　）語 程度まで語彙が増加する

B 【**Comprehension 2**】 Answer the following questions in English.

1. When do babies begin to enjoy babbling?

   ....

2. What is a "vocabulary spurt"?

   ....

3. What do babies often do before saying a word for something?

   ....

C 【**Key Sentences**】 Fill in the blank and translate the following sentences.

⑥ **It is** only after babies turn 12 months old **that** they finally begin to say a few simple words such as "mama" and "mum."

◆ It is 〜 that ... の形は強調構文。only after babies turn 12 months old の部分が強調されている。

訳 : ....

⑦ Their vocabulary continues to grow afterwards, **reaching** about 200 words **in total** at around the age of 24 months.

◆後半は現在分詞 reaching で始まる分詞構文。「〜して，そして…」という「連続」を表している。

◆ in total は「（1.　　　　[日本義で]）」という意味。

訳 : ....

Paragraphs 7～9

教科書 p.58　🔊意味のまとまりに注意して，本文全体を聞こう。 1-46

7　①Some of you may hope / to raise children / with good bilingual skills, / but that can be challenging. // ②This is because a baby's brain is naturally adapted / to its environment. // ③When exposed only to Japanese, / newly-born babies become good / at understanding Japanese. // ④On the other hand, / they will eventually stop distinguishing sounds / such as /l/ and /r/, / which are important to English / but not to Japanese. // ⑤Balancing two languages is a very difficult task. //

8　⑥American psychologist Patricia Kuhl and her colleagues / examined whether English-speaking infants could maintain / their ability / to tell apart two Mandarin sounds. // ⑦Interestingly, / they found / that babies who engaged in interaction / with an actual Mandarin-speaking person / were more likely to maintain / this ability / than others who listened only to Mandarin sounds / from non-interactive audio recordings. // ⑧Babies seem / to find interaction more meaningful and relevant / to their lives. // ⑨This could have a positive influence / on their language development. //

9　⑩These findings suggest / that babies develop their language skills / in order to communicate with people / around them. // ⑪Whether it is a first / or a second language, / such motivation drives our language development. // ⑫What about your learning / of English? // ⑬Who would you like to interact with? // ⑭Little babies may be offering us / a good chance / to reflect on our own language learning. //

🔊意味のまとまりに注意して，本文全体を音読しよう。（210 Words）

Words and Phrases 新出単語・表現の意味を調べよう			
bilingual 形 [baɪlíŋgw(ə)l] B1	1.	challenging 形 [tʃǽlɪn(d)ʒɪŋ] B1	2.
adapt 動 [ədǽpt] B1	3.	expose 動 [ɪkspóuz] B1	4.
be exposed to …	5.	psychologist 名 [saɪká(:)lədʒɪst] A2	6.
Patricia Kuhl [pətríʃə kúːl]	パトリシア・クール	colleague 名 [ká(:)liːg] B2	7.
examine 動 [ɪgzǽmɪn] B1	8.	apart 副 [əpáːrt] A2	9.
tell … apart	10.	Mandarin [mǽnd(ə)rɪn]	北京語

engage 動 [ɪngéɪdʒ] B1	11.	engaged in …	12.
interaction 名 [ìnt(ə)rǽkʃ(ə)n] B1	13.	interactive 形 [ìnt(ə)rǽktɪv] B2	14.
meaningful 形 [míːnɪŋf(ə)l] B1	15.	relevant 形 [rélǝv(ə)nt] B2	16.
be relevant to …	17.		

A 【Comprehension 1】 Fill in the blanks in Japanese.

要点を整理しよう【思考力・判断力・表現力】

赤ちゃんの言語習得の特徴　　（外国語との関係を通して）

赤ちゃんの脳は（1.　　　　　　）に適応する
　日本語だけに接している新生児：日本語の理解はうまくできるようになるが，日本語では重要でない音の（2.　　　　　　）がつかなくなる。

赤ちゃんは対話が重要であり生活と関連があるとわかる
　北京語の音を正しく区別する能力：（3.　　　　　　）された音声だけを聞くよりも，北京語の（4.　　　　　　）と対話をしたほうが能力が維持されやすい。（実験結果）

→赤ちゃんは，周囲の人たちと（5.　　　　　　　　　　）をとるために言語スキルを発達させる。

B 【Comprehension 2】 Answer the following questions in English.

本文のポイントについて答えよう【思考力・判断力・表現力】

1. Why is it challenging to raise children with good bilingual skills?

----

2. What could have a positive influence on the language development of babies?

C 【Key Sentences】 Fill in the blanks and translate the following sentences.

重要文について確認しよう【知識・技能】【思考力・判断力・表現力】

③ **When exposed** only to Japanese, <u>newly-born babies</u> become good at understanding Japanese.
　◆前半は newly-born babies are が省略されている（もしくは接続詞を分詞の前に置いた分詞構文）。
　◆ be exposed to … は「…に（1.　　　　　　[日本語で]）」の意味。
　訳：--

⑪ **Whether** it is a first **or** a second language, **such motivation** drives our language development.
　◆この whether は「譲歩」を表す接続詞。whether A or B で「A であろうと B であろうと」。
　◆ such motivation＝the motivation to（2.　　　　　　[英語 3 語で]）around us
　訳：--

45

Activity Plus 教科書 p.62 🔊意味のまとまりに注意して，本文全体を聞こう。 🎧1-48

①A researcher visits a high school / to give a short lecture / on how to find out / what babies know / or are thinking. // ②Here is the script / of his lecture. //

③Babies cannot explain their understanding / in words. // ④Do you know / how researchers investigate their knowledge? // ⑤Today, / I will talk / about some popular methods / used in baby studies. //

⑥The first method is called a preferential looking test, / which is often used / to determine babies' favorite things. // ⑦Babies tend to look longer / at things / or sources of sounds / they like. // ⑧In an experiment, / for example, / a baby sits on its parent's lap / in a small room, / with a light bulb / on each of the left / and right walls. // ⑨Loudspeakers are built / in behind each light. // ⑩Once the child looks at one of the lights, / a speech stream is played. // ⑪Of course, / each loudspeaker plays a different sound. // ⑫By measuring the looking time, / we can investigate babies' preference. // ⑬I mean, / the longer they look, / the better they like the sound. //

⑭Another common method is a habituation-dishabituation test. // ⑮Babies tend to express interest / in something new, / so we make use of this tendency / when doing an experiment. // ⑯For example, / when a baby is exposed repeatedly / to a certain sound, / the baby gets bored / with it / and eventually no longer looks at the source / of the sound. // ⑰This is called a habituation. // ⑱Then, / a different sound is played. // ⑲If the baby can distinguish the sounds, / it should look again / at the loudspeaker / because, / as I said, / babies like something new. // ⑳This "dishabituation" does not occur / if a baby cannot tell the difference / between the two sounds. //

㉑What other methods / do you think we can use? // ㉒Some researchers create a special pacifier, / which plays a sound / only when babies suck hard. // ㉓Others use an eye tracker / to detect babies' eye positions / and movements. // ㉔As I explained / today, / we need appropriate methods / and techniques / to design reputable baby studies. // ㉕Creativity is one of the keys / we need to use / to unlock the mysteries of / how babies develop. // ㉖Can you come up with any other good methods? //

🔊意味のまとまりに注意して，本文全体を音読しよう。(319 Words)

Words and Phrases 新出単語・表現の意味を調べよう			
lecture 名 [léktʃər] B1	1.	script 名 [skrípt] A2	2.
investigate 動 [ɪnvéstɪgèɪt] B2	3.	preferential 形 [prèfərénʃ(ə)l]	4.

experiment 名 [ɪkspérɪmənt] B1	5.	lap 名 [lǽp] B2	6.
bulb 名 [bʌ́lb] A2	7.	loudspeaker 名 [làudspíːkər] B1	8.
stream 名 [stríːm] B1	9.	be bored with …	10.
habituation 名 [hæbɪtʃuéɪʃ(ə)n]	11.	dishabituation 名 [dìshæbɪtʃuéɪʃ(ə)n]	12.
tendency 名 [téndənsi] B1	13.	repeatedly 副 [rɪpíːtɪdli] B1	14.
pacifier 名 [pǽsɪfàɪər]	15.	tracker 名 [trǽkər]	16.
detect 動 [dɪtékt] B2	17.	reputable 形 [répjətəb(ə)l]	18.
creativity 名 [krìːətívəti] A2	19.	unlock 動 [ʌnlá(ː)k] B2	20.
mystery 名 [míst(ə)ri] A2	21.	come up with …	22.

A 【Comprehension 1】 Fill in the blanks in Japanese.

赤ちゃんに関する研究で用いられる実験

	選好注視法（Preferential Looking Test）	馴化—脱馴化法（Habituation-Dishabituation Test）
目的	赤ちゃんが（1. 　　　　　）音を調べる。	赤ちゃんが音の区別ができるかを調べる。
赤ちゃんの習性	自分の好きなものや音の出るところに長く目を向ける傾向	新しいものに（3. 　　　　　）を示す傾向
方法	部屋の左右の壁に電球とスピーカーを置いて異なる音を流し，赤ちゃんがそれぞれに目を向ける（2. 　　　　　）を測定する。	繰り返して聞こえる音に飽きたころ，それとは異なる音に気づいて赤ちゃんがスピーカーを（4. 　　　　　）かどうか調べる。

B 【Comprehension 2】 Answer the following questions in English.

本文のポイントについて答えよう【思考力・判断力・表現力】

1. If a baby is able to distinguish a different sound after being exposed repeatedly to a certain sound, what can we say has occurred?

----

2. What does the researcher think is essential to unlock the mysteries of baby development?

Paragraphs
1～3　教科書 p.68　🔊意味のまとまりに注意して，本文全体を聞こう。 ◎1-50

①What does it mean / to "go digital"? // ②How will the digital age continue / to develop, / and how will it impact us / and our society? //

1　③What does the word "digital" bring to mind? // ④Some may think / of smartphones, / personal computers / and tablets. // ⑤Others may imagine / e-books, / streaming music, / and online video games. // ⑥These are all electronic, / not quite physical, / and this is one of the important aspects / of going digital. //

2　⑦Digitization refers to the process of changing information / into an electronic format / that can be read / and processed / by a computer. // ⑧A smartphone, / for example, / can work / as a map, / a book / and a watch. // ⑨These things previously existed / as separate physical items, / but now / their contents and functions / have been changed / into digital formats / —— apps. //

3　⑩So, / what happens / when information is digitized? // ⑪Take the example / of digitized documents. // ⑫Digitized documents can go beyond space / and time limitations. // ⑬As they have no physical presence, / they no longer need physical space / for storage. // ⑭They are easier to edit or copy, / and any edits can be easily undone. // ⑮Furthermore, / digitized information can more readily be connected / online. // ⑯These properties can help / make the process and state of things / visible and manageable / virtually / anytime and anywhere. //

🔊意味のまとまりに注意して，本文全体を音読しよう。（179 Words）

Words and Phrases 新出単語・表現の意味を調べよう			
bring … to mind	1.	electronic 形 [ɪlèktrá(:)nɪk] B1	2.
aspect 名 [ǽspekt] B1	3.	digitization 名 [dìdʒɪtaɪzéɪʃ(ə)n]	4.
format 名 [fɔ́ːrmæt] B1	5.	digitize 動 [dídʒɪtàɪz]	6.
document 名 [dá(:)kjəmənt] B1	7.	beyond 前 [biá(:)nd] A2	8.
go beyond …	9.	limitation 名 [lìmɪtéɪʃ(ə)n] B1	10.
presence 名 [préz(ə)ns] B1	11.	edit 動 [édɪt] B2	12.
undone 動 [ʌndʌ́n] B1	undo の過去分詞形	undo 動 [ʌndúː] B1	13.

readily 副 [rédɪli] B2	14.	visible 形 [vízəb(ə)l] B1	15.
manageable 形 [mǽnɪdʒəb(ə)l]	16.	virtually 副 [və́ːrtʃuəli] B2	17.
anytime 副 [énɪtàɪm]	18.		

A 【Comprehension 1】 Fill in the blanks in Japanese.

要点を整理しよう【思考力・判断力・表現力】

> デジタイゼーション ：情報をコンピュータが読み込んだり処理したりすることができる
> 　　　　　　　　　　　（₁.　　　　　　　　）な形式に変換する過程。
> 〔例〕スマートフォン：地図，本，時計など，形のある物から，（₂.　　　　　　　　）というデジタ
> 　　ル形式に変換
> ・デジタイゼーションによってデジタル化された文書は（₃.　　　　　　　　）と時間の制約がない。
> →（₄.　　　　　　　　）のための場所が不要／（₅.　　　　　　　　）や複製が簡単／オンライン上で関
> 　連づけることが容易

B 【Comprehension 2】 Answer the following questions in English.

本文のポイントについて答えよう【思考力・判断力・表現力】

1. What have the functions of maps, books, and watches been changed into?

　- -

2. When are the process and state of things visible and manageable virtually anytime and anywhere?

　- -

C 【Key Sentences】 Fill in the blanks and translate the following sentences.

重要文について確認しよう【知識・技能】【思考力・判断力・表現力】

⑬ **As** they have no physical presence, they no longer need physical space for storage.

　◆接続詞 as は「…なので」というように，理由や原因を表す。
　◆ they＝（₁.　　　　　　　　[英語2語で]）
　訳： -

⑯ **These properties** can help **make** the process and state of things visible and manageable virtually anytime and anywhere.

　◆ these properties は，デジタル化された文書が（₂.　　　　　　　　[日本語で]）や複製が簡単で
　あり，デジタル化された情報が容易に（₃.　　　　　　　　[日本語で]）上で関連づけることができ
　るといった特性。
　◆ make＋O＋C で「O を C にする」。ここでは C が形容詞句で示されている。
　訳： -

Paragraphs
4〜6　教科書 p.69　◀意味のまとまりに注意して，本文全体を聞こう。 1-52

④ ①Digitization concerns changing something / into digital data, / but "digitalization" takes things / a step further. // ②Making use of digital data / and the abilities of various recent technologies, / digitalization entirely changes the process / of doing things. // ③It involves collecting / and analyzing data, / running simulations / and making better decisions / about what to do. //

⑤ ④One of the key digitalized technologies / is the Internet of Things (IoT). // ⑤It allows physical objects / to be connected / online. // ⑥These objects are equipped / with sensors, / cameras, / and other technologies / that help connect / and exchange data / with other devices and systems. // ⑦Cloud technology can remove data storage limitations. // ⑧Also, / AI technologies make it possible / to run precise simulations / based on collected data. //

⑥ ⑨An example of digitalization is / the use of a digital twin. // ⑩It is a virtual replica / of a physical thing, / which can display / what the real one is doing / or is going to do. // ⑪This technology was employed / in the 2018 FIFA World Cup. // ⑫In each match, / the player and ball movements / were tracked / in real time / and were reproduced / digitally. // ⑬The participating teams were allowed / to use the analysis / and simulation results / for their decision-making / during the match. //

　　　　　　　　◀意味のまとまりに注意して，本文全体を音読しよう。（191 Words）

Words and Phrases　新出単語・表現の意味を調べよう			
digitalization 名 [dìdʒɪt(ə)laɪzéɪʃ(ə)n]	1.	involve 動 [ɪnvá(:)lv] B1	2.
simulation 名 [sìmjəléɪʃ(ə)n]	3.	digitalize 動 [dídʒɪt(ə)làɪz]	4.
object 名 [á(:)bdʒekt] B1	5.	equip 動 [ɪkwíp] B2	6.
equip A with B	7.	precise 形 [prɪsáɪs] A2	8.
twin 名 [twín] B1	9.	virtual 形 [vá:rtʃuəl] B1	10.
replica 名 [réplɪkə] B2	11.	employ 動 [ɪmplɔ́ɪ] B2	12.

reproduce 動 [rì:prədjú:s] B1	13.	digitally 副 [dídʒɪt(ə)li]	14.
analysis 名 [ənǽləsɪs] B1	15.		

A 【Comprehension 1】 Fill in the blanks in Japanese.

要点を整理しよう【思考力・判断力・表現力】

> デジタライゼーション ：デジタルデータや技術を用いて，何かをする（1.　　　　　　　）を変化
> 　　　　　　　　　　　　させること
> 　　　　　　　　　①データの収集・分析　②シミュレーション　③よりよい決定
> 〔例〕「モノのインターネット」：物理的なモノをオンラインで接続する
> 　　　・クラウド技術：データの（2.　　　　　　）の容量制限の除去
> 　　　・AI 技術：収集されたデータをもとにした（3.　　　　　　）なシミュレーション
> 〔例〕デジタルツイン：物理的なモノを（4.　　　　　　）上に複製したもの
> 　　　↑　　　2018年 FIFA ワールドカップで，参加チームは試合中の（5.　　　　　　　　）
> 　　　　　　のために使用することが認められた

B 【Comprehension 2】 Answer the following questions in English.

本文のポイントについて答えよう【思考力・判断力・表現力】

1. What does digitalization use when it changes the process of doing things?

   ----

2. What did the participating teams use a digital twin for in the 2018 FIFA World Cup?

C 【Key Sentences】 Fill in the blanks and translate the following sentences.

重要文について確認しよう【知識・技能】【思考力・判断力・表現力】

② **Making** use of digital data and the abilities of various recent technologies, digitalization entirely changes the process of doing things.

   ◆現在分詞 making で始まる分詞構文で「同時（付帯状況）」を表す。

   ◆ make use of ... は「…を（1.　　　　　　　[日本語で]）」の意味。

   訳：--

⑧ Also, AI technologies **make** it possible to **run** precise simulations based on collected data.

   ◆ make O＋C で「O を C にする」。it＝（2.　　　　　　　[英語8語で]）

   ◆ run は他動詞で，「（プログラムなど）を動かす」の意味。

   訳：--

Paragraphs 7～9 教科書 p.70 ◁意味のまとまりに注意して，本文全体を聞こう。◎1-54

⑦ ①When the use of digital technologies affects society / and human activity, / it is called "digital transformation (DX)." // ②In education, / for example, / DX may drastically change / how teaching and learning take place. // ③Students' learning data / is automatically collected / in digital form / all the time. // ④Based on that information, / the most suitable study content / and plans / can be suggested, / enabling both teachers and learners / to create a more effective / and engaging educational process. //

⑧ ⑤DX also impacts the notion / of shopping / and our behavior / as consumers. // ⑥Online shopping has brought about virtual shopping. // ⑦Personalized recommendations / on a shopping website / constitute the digitalization / of what a salesclerk used to do / in the physical shop. // ⑧The lines / between digital and in-store shopping experiences / are becoming less clear / than they were / before. //

⑨ ⑨Promoting digitization, / digitalization / or digital transformation / is not necessarily easy, / however. // ⑩In the business world, / companies and organizations cannot afford / to provide training / for their employees / to cover all of the necessary digital skills. // ⑪Transforming the existing systems / into digital ones / could be heavily constrained / if they are too complex / and are already "black boxes." // ⑫Still, / going digital seems / to be an inevitable trend. // ⑬How far are we now / from a fully digital world? //

◁意味のまとまりに注意して，本文全体を音読しよう。（200 Words）

Words and Phrases 新出単語・表現の意味を調べよう			
transformation 名 [trænsfərméɪʃ(ə)n] B1	1.	educational 形 [èdʒəkéɪʃ(ə)n(ə)l] A2	2.
bring about …	3.	personalize 動 [pə́ːrs(ə)nəlàɪz]	4.
recommendation 名 [rèkəmendéɪʃ(ə)n] B2	5.	salesclerk 名 [séɪlzklə̀ːrk]	6.
afford 動 [əfɔ́ːrd] B1	7.	cannot afford to ～	8.
provide A for B	9.	employee 名 [ɪmplɔ́ːiː] B2	10.
transform 動 [trænsfɔ́ːrm] B1	11.	transform A into B	12.

constrain 動 [kənstréin]	13.	complex 形 [kà(:)mpléks] B1	14.
inevitable 形 [mévɪtəb(ə)l] B1	15.	far from …	16.

A 【**Comprehension 1**】 Fill in the blanks in Japanese.

要点を整理しよう【思考力・判断力・表現力】

> デジタル・トランスフォーメーション ：デジタル技術の使用によって，（1.   ）や
> （2.   ）の活動に影響を与えること
> 〔例〕①教育の分野：最適な学習内容や学習（3.   ）の提案→効果的で魅力的な教育の
> 過程
> ②買い物：オンラインショッピング→（4.   ）に合わせたおすすめ

※デジタル化の推進は必ずしも（5.   ）ではない。

〔例〕ビジネスの世界：デジタルスキルのすべての訓練の提供や，複雑な現存のシステムを転換することの制約

B 【**Comprehension 2**】 Answer the following questions in English.

本文のポイントについて答えよう【思考力・判断力・表現力】

1. As a result of digital transformation in education, what can teachers and learners do?

2. What is happening to the lines between digital and in-store shopping experiences?

3. What is the "black box"?

C 【**Key Sentences**】 Fill in the blanks and translate the following sentences.

重要文について確認しよう【知識・技能】【思考力・判断力・表現力】

⑦ Personalized recommendations on a shopping website constitute the digitalization of **what a salesclerk used to do** in the physical shop.

◆ what は関係代名詞で，of の目的語となる名詞句をつくる。used to ～は過去の習慣や状態を表す。
what a salesclerk used to do で「店員が（1.   [日本語で]）こと」。

訳 :

⑪ Transforming the existing systems into **digital ones** could be heavily constrained if they are too complex and are already "black boxes."

◆ Transforming で始まる動名詞句がこの文の主語。digital ones＝digital（2.   [英語1語で]）

訳 :

Activity Plus 教科書p.74 ◀意味のまとまりに注意して，本文全体を聞こう。 ◎1-56

①You are looking for some information / about going paperless / on the Internet / and have found the following blog post / about the positive aspects / of paper use. //

②Going paperless will bring us / a lot of benefits. // ③However, / that doesn't mean / we should stop using paper / completely. // ④There seem to be positive aspects / of paper / that should be noted. //

⑤First of all, / paper is simple / and easy to use. // ⑥Even a small child can understand / how to use it. // ⑦Also, / paper does not require devices / or electricity. // ⑧To use digital data, / some sort of digital device, / such as a computer / or a tablet, / is a must. // ⑨Without an electronic device, / digital data can never be read / or created. //

⑩Another good point about paper is / that it can be enjoyed / through the senses. // ⑪You can feel its roughness / or smoothness / and its smell. // ⑫If you write something / on it, / you can feel / its unique touch. // ⑬In these respects, / paper is more real / to us. // ⑭At present, / however, / it is impossible / for digital technology / to replicate / such experiences. //

⑮Paper may be better / for your eyes, / particularly when you read / (or write) something / for a long time. // ⑯Due to their brightness / and glare, / digital screens can cause / more eye strain and fatigue / than reading from a paper page. // ⑰For this reason, / there are definitely some people / who still prefer paper / to screen. //

⑱Reading from paper can facilitate / better understanding / for the learner. // ⑲As it is friendly / to your eyes, / more time may be spent / on concentrated / and in-depth reading. // ⑳The fatiguing nature of digital on-screen reading / can lead / to non-linear selective reading, / which could consequently decrease / sustained attention / to the text. //

㉑I believe / paper still holds an essential place / in this digital age / and is here / to stay. // ◀意味のまとまりに注意して，本文全体を音読しよう。(267 Words)

Words and Phrases 新出単語・表現の意味を調べよう			
paperless 形 [péɪpərləs] B2	1.	first of all	2.
roughness 名 [rʌ́fnəs]	3.	smoothness 名 [smúːðnəs]	4.
at present	5.	replicate 動 [répləkèɪt]	6.

brightness 名 [bráɪtnəs]	7.	strain 名 [stréɪn] B1	8.
prefer 動 [prɪfə́:r] A2	9.	prefer A to B	10.
concentrate 動 [ká(:)ns(ə)ntrèɪt] A2	11.	in-depth 形 [ìndépθ]	12.
fatiguing 形 [fətí:gɪŋ]	13.	selective 形 [səléktɪv]	14.
consequently 副 [ká(:)nsəkwèntli] B1	15.	sustain 動 [səstéɪn] B2	16.
text 名 [tékst] A2	17.		

A 【Comprehension 1】 Fill in the blanks in Japanese.

要点を整理しよう【思考力・判断力・表現力】

紙の文書の長所

①単純で使いやすい ・小さな子供でもその (1.　　　　) を理解できる ・機器や (2.　　　　) を必要としない	②感覚を通じて楽しむことができる ・紙の粗さや (3.　　　　)，匂いを感じることができる ・より (4.　　　　) な体験を生み出す
③目によい ・明るさや (5.　　　　) がない ・目と身体の (6.　　　　) が少ない	④学習者の理解を促進する ・長い (7.　　　　) にわたって集中して綿密に読むことができる ・文書に (8.　　　　) 的に注意を向けられる

B 【Comprehension 2】 Answer the following questions in English.

本文のポイントについて答えよう【思考力・判断力・表現力】

1. According to the blog post, what is needed to use digital data?

---

2. According to the blog post, why can digital screens cause eye strain and fatigue?

C 【Key Sentence】 Translate the following sentence.

重要文について確認しよう【知識・技能】【思考力・判断力・表現力】

④ There seem to be <u>positive aspects of paper</u> (**that** should be noted).

◆ There seem to be ... で「…があるようだ」。続く名詞が単数形であれば There seems to be ... とする。

◆ that で始まる関係代名詞の節が直前の positive aspects of paper を修飾している。

訳:

Paragraphs 1〜3

◖意味のまとまりに注意して，本文全体を聞こう。 1-58

①Some of you may remember / the year 2020 / as a bad one / for public health. // ②When looking into our past, / we realize / that people in the past experienced / similar health crises. // ③They might have had the same feelings / as you did. //

1 ④The World Health Organization, / or WHO, / declared the COVID-19 infections / a pandemic / on March 12, 2020. // ⑤In fact, / this was not the first time / that human beings combatted / infectious diseases / on a global stage. // ⑥We have a very long history / of fighting against them. // ⑦With changes / in the global environment / and human behavior, / various diseases and sicknesses have come / and gone. //

2 ⑧Infectious diseases are illnesses / caused by microorganisms / such as bacteria, / viruses / or parasites. // ⑨Many of them / live in and on our bodies, / and are normally harmless / or sometimes even beneficial. // ⑩Under certain conditions, / however, / some organisms may cause diseases. // ⑪Bacteria are relatively complex, / single-cell creatures, / and they can reproduce / on their own. // ⑫In contrast, / a virus cannot survive / without a host. // ⑬It is always looking for a place / to leave its offspring. // ⑭When a virus enters the human body / and reproduces, / it causes harm. //

3 ⑮People have been fighting / against infectious diseases / since ancient times. // ⑯According to some researchers, / examinations of Egyptian mummies / have shown / that those people suffered / from various diseases / and parasites. // ⑰As one example, / the eggs of disease-carrying parasites / that came from eating snails / were found / in some mummies. //

◖意味のまとまりに注意して，本文全体を音読しよう。（192 Words）

Words and Phrases 新出単語・表現の意味を調べよう			
declare 動 [dɪkléər] B1	1.	infection 名 [ɪnfékʃ(ə)n] B1	2.
pandemic 名 [pændémɪk]	3.	combat 動 [kɑ́(:)mbæt]	4.
come and go	5.	microorganism 名 [màɪkrouɔ́:rɡənìz(ə)m] B2	6.
virus 名 [váɪ(ə)rəs] B1	7.	parasite 名 [pǽrəsàɪt]	8.
harmless 形 [hɑ́:rmləs] B2	9.	organism 名 [ɔ́:rɡənìz(ə)m] B1	10.
relatively 副 [rélətɪvli] B1	11.	cell 名 [sél] B1	12.

offspring 名 [ɔ́ːfsprìŋ]	13.	harm 名 [háːrm] A2	14.
Egyptian 形 [ɪdʒípʃ(ə)n]	15.	mummy 名 [mʌ́mi]	16.
snail 名 [snéɪl]	17.		

A 【Comprehension 1】 Fill in the blanks in Japanese.

要点を整理しよう【思考力・判断力・表現力】

感染症 ← 微生物
・多くが人間の体内や体表に生息
・通常は無害で,（1.　　　　　）なものもある

細菌	比較的複雑な (2.　　　　　) 生物。自分自身で (3.　　　　　) できる。
ウイルス	(4.　　　　　) がなければ生存できない。 →人体に侵入して繁殖すると害をおよぼす。

古来より<u>人間が戦ってきた</u>
〔証拠〕エジプトの (5.　　　　　)：体内から病気を運ぶ寄生虫の卵が見つかる

B 【Comprehension 2】 Answer the following questions in English.

本文のポイントについて答えよう【思考力・判断力・表現力】

1. What did the World Health Organization do on March 12, 2020?

2. What does a virus need to survive?

C 【Key Sentences】 Fill in the blanks and translate the following sentences.

重要文について確認しよう【知識・技能】【思考力・判断力・表現力】

⑤ In fact, **this** was not the first time (**that** human beings combatted infectious diseases on a global stage).

◆ this は「COVID-19によってもたらされた（1.　　　　[日本語で]）」のこと。
◆関係代名詞 that の節が直前の the first time を修飾している。

訳:

⑯ According to some researchers, examinations of Egyptian mummies have shown that **those people** suffered from various diseases and parasites.

◆ those people は「古代エジプトの（2.　　　　[日本語で]）となった人々」のこと。

訳:

Paragraphs 4～6

教科書 p.81　◁意味のまとまりに注意して，本文全体を聞こう。◉1-60

4 ①Infectious diseases are mirrors of the times / ── they have changed their forms / according to people's lifestyles / of the time. // ②When the earliest humans began to settle / on riversides, / sharing the river water / caused epidemics / of digestive diseases. // ③When people started / to gather / in cities / and live closer together, / illnesses could be transmitted / more easily / from person to person. // ④When cities became larger, / there were no sewage systems / in the beginning, / and diseases spread / through human waste. //

5 ⑤In response to the spread of diseases, / people have transformed / social systems. // ⑥In big cities / of Europe / in the 14th century, / a large number of rats / spread the plague bacteria. // ⑦This plague pandemic was responsible / for killing an estimated 60 percent / of Europe's entire population. // ⑧The spread of the disease / caused the social structure / to change significantly, / which, / on the bright side, / led to the liberation / of people / and the Renaissance era. //

6 ⑨Four centuries later / during the Industrial Revolution, / many factories were built / and people migrated / from rural areas / to cities / to work. // ⑩They had to work hard / and were poorly nourished, / which made many of them sick. // ⑪Tuberculosis soon became epidemic. // ⑫Protesting against their bad working conditions, / many workers, / including children, / set up unions / and fought against their employers. // ⑬They succeeded / in improving their working and living conditions. // ◁意味のまとまりに注意して，本文全体を音読しよう。(216 Words)

Words and Phrases 新出単語・表現の意味を調べよう			
settle 動 [sét(ə)l] B1	1.	riverside 名 [rívərsàɪd]	2.
epidemic 名 [èpɪdémɪk]	3.	digestive 形 [daɪdʒéstɪv]	4.
transmit 動 [trænsmít] B2	5.	in response to …	6.
plague 名 [pléɪg] B2	7.	be responsible for …	8.
significantly 副 [sɪgnífɪk(ə)ntli] B2	9.	on the bright side	10.
liberation 名 [lìbəréɪʃ(ə)n] B1	11.	Renaissance 形 [rènəsáːns]	12.
industrial 形 [ɪndʌ́striəl] B1	13.	revolution 名 [rèvəlúːʃ(ə)n] B2	14.

tuberculosis 名 [tjubə̀ːrkjəlóusəs] B2	15.	employer 名 [ɪmplɔ́ɪər] B2	16.

A 【Comprehension 1】 Fill in the blanks in Japanese.

要点を整理しよう【思考力・判断力・表現力】

感染症は時代を映す
(1.　　　　　) ＝感染症はその時代の人々の（2.　　　　　）によってその姿を変えてきた。

人々の生活様式と感染症の関係
　　①川岸の定住〔川の水の共有による（3.　　　　　）系の病気の流行〕　→　②都市の形成
　　〔人から人への伝染〕　→　③都市の拡大〔人間の（4.　　　　　）を介した病気の蔓延〕
感染症による社会システムの変革
　　14世紀：ペストの大流行　⇒人々の（5.　　　　　）運動，ルネサンス時代
　　18世紀：結核の大流行　⇒（6.　　　　　）の結成　⇒労働条件・生活環境の改善

B 【Comprehension 2】 Answer the following questions in English.

本文のポイントについて答えよう【思考力・判断力・表現力】

1. When the earliest humans began to settle on riversides, why did epidemics of digestive diseases happen?

　　--

2. Where and when did the plague pandemic happen?

　　--

3. What did many workers do to protest against their bad working conditions?

　　--

C 【Key Sentences】 Fill in the blank and translate the following sentences.

重要文について確認しよう【知識・技能】【思考力・判断力・表現力】

⑧ The spread of the disease **caused** the social structure **to** change significantly, **which** (, on the bright side,) led to the liberation of people and the Renaissance era.

　◆ cause A to ～で「A に～させる」という意味。
　◆関係代名詞 which の非制限用法。前の節全体が先行詞となっている。on the bright side は挿入句。
　訳: --

　　--

⑫ **Protesting** against their bad working conditions, many workers, including children, set up unions and fought against their employers.

　◆現在分詞 protesting で始まる分詞構文。意味上の主語は（1.　　　　　[英語2語で]）。
　訳: --

　　--

Paragraphs 7〜9

教科書 p.82　🔊意味のまとまりに注意して，本文全体を聞こう。　◎1-62

7　①Thanks to the work / of many researchers and physicians, / we now have ways / to fight against infectious diseases. // ②One is vaccination. // ③By being injected / with a weaker form of the virus / before contracting the real one, / people can increase immunity / against the disease / it causes. // ④The French chemist / Louis Pasteur / developed this technique / for preventing rabies / in 1881. //

8　⑤Another method is / taking medication, / which can kill or weaken / the virus or bacteria / in the body. // ⑥For example, / in 1928, / penicillin was discovered / by Alexander Fleming, / a Scottish physician-scientist. // ⑦It is a type of antibiotic, / which prevents the growth / of bacteria / or kills them. //

9　⑧Adjusting our ways of life / to the circumstances / in which a disease occurs / may be another solution. // ⑨In the 19th century, / people finally discovered / that the cause of plague / was their unclean sanitary conditions. // ⑩They constructed a sewage system / and began / to use it. // ⑪This story may remind you / of the WHO's declaration / of a pandemic / in 2020, / which caused our lifestyles / to change. // ⑫Like the people of the past, / you may find it hard / to change your habits, / but getting used to a new lifestyle / and finding its beneficial aspects / may be the key / to living happy / and healthy lives. //

🔊意味のまとまりに注意して，本文全体を音読しよう。(204 Words)

Words and Phrases 新出単語・表現の意味を調べよう			
physician 名 [fɪzíʃ(ə)n] B2	1.	vaccination 名 [væksɪnéɪʃ(ə)n]	2.
inject 動 [ɪndʒékt] B1	3.	contract 動 [kəntrǽkt]	4.
immunity 名 [ɪmjú:nəti]	5.	chemist 名 [kémɪst] B1	6.
Louis Pasteur [lú:i pæstə́:r]	ルイ・パスツール	rabies 名 [réɪbi:z]	7.
medication 名 [mèdɪkéɪʃ(ə)n] B2	8.	weaken 動 [wí:k(ə)n] B2	9.
penicillin 名 [pènəsílɪn] B2	10.	Alexander Fleming [æ̀lɪgzǽndər flémɪŋ]	アレクサンダー・フレミング
Scottish 形 [ská(:)tɪʃ]	11.	antibiotic 名 [æ̀ntibaɪá(:)tɪk]	12.
adjust 動 [ədʒʌ́st] A2	13.	adjust A to B	14.

| circumstance 名
[sə́ːrkəmstæns] B2 | 15. | sanitary 形
[sǽnətèri] B2 | 16. |
| declaration 名
[dèkləréɪʃ(ə)n] B1 | 17. | get used to … | 18. |

A 【**Comprehension 1**】 Fill in the blanks in Japanese.

要点を整理しよう【思考力・判断力・表現力】

現代の私たちが感染症に立ち向かう方法

ワクチン接種	弱くしたウイルスを注射して，（1.　　　　　　）を高める。 〔例〕（2.　　　　　　）のワクチン接種：1881年にルイ・パスツールが開発
薬	体内の（3.　　　　　　）や（4.　　　　　　）を死滅させたり弱体化させたりする。 〔例〕ペニシリン：1928年にアレクサンダー・フレミングが発見
生活様式の適合	病気が発生している環境に合わせて生活様式を適合させる。 〔例〕（5.　　　　　　）の整備

B 【**Comprehension 2**】 Answer the following questions in English.

本文のポイントについて答えよう【思考力・判断力・表現力】

1. How can people increase immunity against the disease the virus causes?

2. Who was Alexander Fleming?

C 【**Key Sentences**】 Fill in the blanks and translate the following sentences.

重要文について確認しよう【知識・技能】【思考力・判断力・表現力】

③ By **being injected** with a weaker form of the virus before contracting the real **one**, people can increase immunity against the disease (**it** causes).

◆〈being＋過去分詞〉は受動態の動名詞。being injected で「注射をされること」。
◆it causes は直前の the disease を修飾している。関係代名詞 which が省略されている。
◆ one と it はともに the（1.　　　[英語1語で]）を指す。

訳：

⑧ Adjusting our ways of life to the circumstances (**in which** a disease occurs) may be another solution.

◆〈前置詞＋関係代名詞〉の in which が導く節が直前の the circumstances を修飾している。
◆この文の述語動詞は（2.　　　[英語1語で]）。

訳：

Activity Plus 教科書 p.86 ◁意味のまとまりに注意して，本文全体を聞こう。 ◉1-64

①You are studying / about the history / of infectious diseases. // ②You found the story / of Louis Pasteur. //

③In the 1880s, / rabies met its match / in a French scientist / named Louis Pasteur. // ④In 1881, / all Pasteur knew for certain / was that the disease was carried / to humans / in the saliva / of rabid animals. // ⑤He figured / that the germ had to travel / from the bite / to the victim's brain / and spinal cord. // ⑥After identifying the germ, / he was able to develop a vaccine. // ⑦Finally, / he proved / it was effective / on an animal / attacked by a rabid animal. //

⑧But would the vaccine also prove effective / on humans? // ⑨Pasteur was reluctant / to try it. // ⑩What if Pasteur injected a person / with the rabies vaccine / and gave him the disease / instead of curing him? // ⑪There was only one thing for him to do: / test the vaccine / on himself. //

⑫As Pasteur made preparations / for this drastic step, / a nine-year-old boy / named Joseph / and his mother came / to his office. // ⑬The boy had just been viciously attacked / by a rabid dog / on his way to school. // ⑭But his mother was focused / not on his wounds / but on the possibility / of rabies. //

⑮Pasteur pointed out / the grave risks involved. // ⑯But the mother pleaded with Pasteur / to save him. // ⑰Since Pasteur wasn't a medical doctor, / he had to ask doctors / to examine Joseph's wounds. // ⑱They urged Pasteur / to use his vaccine. // ⑲Pasteur decided to take the risk. //

⑳On the first day, / Pasteur injected Joseph / with a very mild form / of the germ. // ㉑Each day, / he gave the boy / a slightly stronger dose. // ㉒On the 14th day, / Pasteur injected Joseph / with a very powerful dose. // ㉓Joseph, / however, / showed no signs / of the disease. //

㉔Still, / Pasteur had to wait and watch. // ㉕Perhaps / the rabies was just taking its time / to reach the boy's spinal cord / and brain. // ㉖But as each day passed / with no sign of disease, / Pasteur's hopes rose. // ㉗Joseph might live! // ㉘Not only would that be a personal victory / for Pasteur and the boy, / but it would signal / that the disease was finally conquered. // ㉙In August, / Pasteur was finally convinced. // ㉚"It has been 31 days / since Joseph was bitten," / he wrote / in his notebook. // ㉛"He is now quite safe. // ㉜The vaccine is successful." //

◁意味のまとまりに注意して，本文全体を音読しよう。（357 Words)

Words and Phrases 新出単語・表現の意味を調べよう			
for certain	1.	saliva 图 [səláɪvə]	2.

rabid 形 [rǽbɪd]	3.	germ 名 [dʒə́ːrm] B2	4.
spinal 形 [spáɪn(ə)l]	5.	vaccine 名 [væksíːn] B2	6.
reluctant 形 [rɪlʌ́kt(ə)nt] B2	7.	be reluctant to 〜	8.
cure 動 [kjúər] B2	9.	drastic 形 [drǽstɪk]	10.
Joseph [dʒóuzəf]	ジョゼフ	viciously 副 [víʃəsli]	11.
wound 名 [wúːnd] B1	12.	point out …	13.
grave 形 [gréɪv]	14.	plead 動 [plíːd] B2	15.
plead with …	16.	urge 動 [ə́ːrdʒ] B2	17.
urge … to 〜	18.	mild 形 [máɪld] B1	19.
slightly 副 [sláɪtli] B1	20.	dose 名 [dóus] B2	21.

A 【Comprehension 1】 Fill in the blanks in Japanese.

要点を整理しよう【思考力・判断力・表現力】

ルイ・パスツールの狂犬病ワクチン開発

狂犬病のワクチンを開発し，（1.　　　　　　）に対する効果を証明する。

→

そのワクチンの（2.　　　　　　）に対する有効性を証明するために，（3.　　　　　　）の体を使って実験する準備を進める。

→

狂犬病を持った（4.　　　　　　）にかまれた少年ジョゼフと母親がやってくる。

↓

31日目に症状が出なかったことをもって，ワクチンが（7.　　　　　）したことを確信する。

←

病原菌を非常に弱いものから徐々に強めながら接種し，（6.　　　　）日目に非常に強力な投薬をする。

←

（5.　　　　　　）の助言により，ジョゼフにワクチンを使用することを決める。

B 【Comprehension 2】 Answer the following questions in English.

本文のポイントについて答えよう【思考力・判断力・表現力】

1. Why was Pasteur reluctant to inject a person with the rabies vaccine he developed?

2. What did doctors do to save Joseph?

Paragraphs 1～3

教科書 p.92　🔊意味のまとまりに注意して，本文全体を聞こう。 2-2

①Eating well / is an essential part of athletes' training / which has gained attention / recently. // ②Let's learn about sports nutrition. //

1　③During the New Year season, / many people watch the Tokyo-Hakone Collegiate "Ekiden" Road Relay. // ④Teams of university students leave Tokyo, / running to Hakone and back / over two days. // ⑤Each team member covers a segment / of the total distance. // ⑥As Hakone is a mountainous area / and the round-trip distance is a long 217.9 kilometers, / this popular race is regarded / as one of the most challenging races / in Japan. //

2　⑦In 2012, / Toyo University won first prize, / setting a race record. // ⑧It was true / that all members of the team / were competent runners, / but they also had a secret weapon / that supported their efforts: / Professor Kazuhiro Uenishi / and his students / at Kagawa Nutrition University. // ⑨They analyzed each runner's nutritional condition / by examining their blood / and measuring their body-fat percentage / and bone density. // ⑩They also developed a meal menu / for each runner / to build a fit and strong body. // ⑪During a few days / just before the race, / they made meals / for the team. //

3　⑫Professor Uenishi has been giving some guidance / on nutrition / to other teams and athletes / in a variety of sports. // ⑬There are some points / athletes should keep in mind / concerning what and how they eat. // ⑭Let's take a look at each point. //

🔊意味のまとまりに注意して，本文全体を音読しよう。（200 Words）

Words and Phrases 新出単語・表現の意味を調べよう			
collegiate 形 [kəlí:dʒiət]	1.	relay 名 [rí:leɪ] B2	2.
segment 名 [ségmənt] B2	3.	regard A as B	4.
competent 形 [ká(:)mpət(ə)nt] B2	5.	nutritional 形 [nju:tríʃ(ə)n(ə)l]	6.
percentage 名 [pərséntɪdʒ] B2	7.	density 名 [dénsəti]	8.
guidance 名 [gáɪd(ə)ns] B1	9.	concerning 前 [kənsə́:rnɪŋ] B2	10.
take a look at ...	11.		

A 【Comprehension 1】 Fill in the blanks in Japanese.

要点を整理しよう【思考力・判断力・表現力】

> 東京箱根間往復大学駅伝競走（箱根駅伝）――――（3.　　　　）年に東洋大学が優勝
> ・大学生のチームが東京・箱根間を（1.　　　）
> 日間かけて往復する（217.9キロメートル）
> ⇒日本で最も（2.　　　　　）しがいのある
> レースのひとつ

> 上西一弘教授と学生（女子栄養大学）
> ・ランナーの（4.　　　　）状態の分析
> ・ランナーの（5.　　　　　）の開発, 調理

B 【Comprehension 2】 Answer the following questions in English.

本文のポイントについて答えよう【思考力・判断力・表現力】

1. Why is the Tokyo-Hakone Collegiate "Ekiden" Road Relay regarded as one of the most challenging races in Japan?

2. Who provided the runners from Toyo University with nutritional support in 2012?

3. How was each runner's nutritional condition analyzed?

C 【Key Sentences】 Fill in the blanks and translate the following sentences.

重要文について確認しよう【知識・技能】【思考力・判断力・表現力】

④ Teams of university students leave Tokyo, **running** to Hakone and back over two days.

◆現在分詞 running 以降は分詞構文。主節で表す動詞 leave と動作が連続して起こっていることを表す。
◆ run to Hakone and back は「箱根まで（1.　　　　[日本語で]）で走る」という意味。
訳：

⑬ There are some points (athletes should keep in mind **concerning** what and how they eat).

◆ athletes … eat は直前の some points を修飾している。関係代名詞 which が省略されている。
◆ concerning は前置詞。その目的語に what and how they eat がきている。「彼らが（2.　　　　　[日本語で]）食べるか」の意味。what they eat と how they eat の疑問詞の部分が等位接続詞 and で結ばれている。
訳：

Paragraphs 4〜6

教科書 p.93 📢意味のまとまりに注意して，本文全体を聞こう。2-4

④ ①First, / it's important / to eat three meals / a day. // ②If you skip breakfast, / your body will suffer / from lack of nutrition. // ③If you skip dinner, / your muscles will not be repaired / and get weaker. // ④Sugar quickly changes / to an energy source / for your brain and muscles. // ⑤It is contained / in staple foods / such as rice, / bread / or pasta. // ⑥Eating three meals a day / is the basis of a healthy diet. //

⑤ ⑦Second, / you should add / main and side dishes, / fruits / and dairy products / to the staple food. // ⑧The main dish should be one / like steak / or baked fish, / and the side dish should be salad / or vegetables. // ⑨In this way, / you can take in / almost all of the nutrients / your body needs. // ⑩When you want to eat pasta dishes / or pizza, / adding side dishes and dairy products / will make your meal / healthier. //

⑥ ⑪Third, / for people who play sports, / it's essential / to supplement nutrition / by eating between meals. // ⑫Athletes often use up / lots of energy / and need sugar. // ⑬You may think of high-energy foods / such as potato chips / and chocolate, / but rice balls / and fruits / might be better alternatives. //

📢意味のまとまりに注意して，本文全体を音読しよう。(187 Words)

Words and Phrases 新出単語・表現の意味を調べよう			
skip 動 [skíp] B2	1.	muscle 名 [mʌ́s(ə)l] B1	2.
staple 形 [stéɪp(ə)l]	3.	dairy 形 [déəri]	4.
take in …	5.	nutrient 名 [njúːtriənt] B1	6.
supplement 動 [sʌ́plɪmənt]	7.	use up …	8.
chip 形 [tʃíp] B2	9.		

A 【Comprehension 1】 Fill in the blanks in Japanese.

要点を整理しよう【思考力・判断力・表現力】

スポーツ栄養における3つの重要な点

1	<u>1日3食を食べること</u> ・食事を抜くと栄養不足や（1.　　　　　　）の弱化につながる ・糖質は（2.　　　　　　）に含まれており，すばやく脳や筋肉のエネルギー源となる
2	<u>主食に主菜，副菜，果物，（3.　　　　　　）を加えること</u> ・主菜はステーキや焼き魚など，副菜はサラダや野菜がよい ・身体が必要とする（4.　　　　　　）のほぼすべてを取り入れることができる
3	<u>間食で栄養を補うこと</u> ・スポーツ選手は大量のエネルギーを使い，糖質を必要としている ・（5.　　　　　　）や果物がよい

B 【Comprehension 2】 Answer the following questions in English.

本文のポイントについて答えよう【思考力・判断力・表現力】

1. What happens to sugar in a human body?

   ....

2. If we want to take in almost all of the nutrients our body needs, what should we do?

   ....

3. What examples are mentioned as foods people who play sports should eat between meals?

   ....

C 【Key Sentences】 Fill in the blanks and translate the following sentences.

重要文について確認しよう【知識・技能】【思考力・判断力・表現力】

⑦ Second, you should **add** <u>main and side dishes</u>, <u>fruits</u> and <u>dairy products</u> **to**
　　　　　　　　　　　　　　　　　 [1]　　　　　　　 [2]　　　　　 [3]
the staple food.

　◆ add A to B で「A を B に加える」という意味。A には3種類が列挙されている。[1] は（1.
　　［英語2語で］）と（2.　　　　　　　　　　［英語2語で］）をまとめた表現。

訳：..

⑨ In this way, you can take in **almost all** of <u>the nutrients</u> (your body needs).

　◆ almost all は「ほとんどすべて」という意味。almost all of ... =（3.　　　　　［英語1語で］）of ...。
　◆ your body needs は直前の the nutrients を修飾している。関係代名詞 which が省略されている。

訳：..

Paragraphs 7～9

教科書 p.94 ◁意味のまとまりに注意して，本文全体を聞こう。 ◎2-6

7　①It is also important / to choose foods / for sports nutrition / depending on the intended purpose. // ②In order to strengthen muscles, / athletes should take in / one to two grams of protein / per kilogram of their body weight. // ③Beef, / chicken, / and fish / such as tuna and bonito / contain lots of protein. // ④Sugar is also important / for muscles. // ⑤If our body runs short / of sugar, / it will extract energy / from protein / instead. // ⑥That will result in weakened muscles. //

8　⑦For strengthening bones / in order to prevent injuries, / athletes need plenty / of calcium. // ⑧Calcium tends to be lost / through sweating, / but vitamin K helps bones / take it in. // ⑨Vitamin D also encourages our body / to absorb calcium / and deactivates so-called bone-destroying cells. // ⑩Calcium is found / in milk / and other dairy products. // ⑪Vitamin K is plentiful / in *natto* / and green-leaf vegetables. // ⑫Mushrooms and fish / such as sardines / are excellent sources / of vitamin D. //

9　⑬When Professor Uenishi's students graduated / from university, / they said, / "By managing the nutritional states / of runners, / we gained a sense / of responsibility / for supplying nutritious meals. // ⑭Food is the basis / of human life." // ⑮Human bodies are made / from what we eat. // ⑯Proper daily meals are sure / to make your body / strong and healthy. //

◁意味のまとまりに注意して，本文全体を音読しよう。（200 Words）

Words and Phrases 新出単語・表現の意味を調べよう			
intend 動 [ɪnténd] B1	1.	strengthen 動 [stréŋ(k)θ(ə)n] B1	2.
gram 名 [grǽm] A2	3.	tuna 名 [tjúːnə] B1	4.
bonito 名 [bəníːtoʊ]	5.	run short of …	6.
extract 動 [ɪkstrǽkt] B2	7.	plenty 名 [plénti] A2	8.
plenty of …	9.	calcium 名 [kǽlsiəm]	10.
sweat 動 [swét] A2	11.	vitamin 名 [váɪtəmɪn] B2	12.
absorb 動 [əbzɔ́ːrb] B1	13.	deactivate 動 [diǽktɪvèɪt]	14.
plentiful 形 [pléntɪf(ə)l]	15.	sardine 名 [sàːrdíːn]	16.

manage 動 [mǽnɪdʒ] A2	17.	be sure to ～	18.

A 【Comprehension 1】 Fill in the blanks in Japanese.

要点を整理しよう【思考力・判断力・表現力】

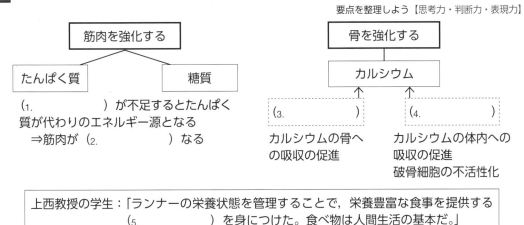

筋肉を強化する
├ たんぱく質
└ 糖質

(1.　　　　　) が不足するとたんぱく質が代わりのエネルギー源となる
⇒筋肉が（2.　　　　　）なる

骨を強化する
└ カルシウム
　↑ (3.　　　　　)
　↑ (4.　　　　　)

カルシウムの骨への吸収の促進

カルシウムの体内への吸収の促進
破骨細胞の不活性化

上西教授の学生：「ランナーの栄養状態を管理することで，栄養豊富な食事を提供する（5.　　　　　）を身につけた。食べ物は人間生活の基本だ。」

B 【Comprehension 2】 Answer the following questions in English.

本文のポイントについて答えよう【思考力・判断力・表現力】

1. What will our body do if it runs short of sugar?

2. What examples are mentioned as foods which can help us strengthen bones?

3. How did Professor Uenishi's students gain a sense of responsibility for supplying nutritious meals?

C 【Key Sentences】 Fill in the blanks and translate the following sentences.

重要文について確認しよう【知識・技能】【思考力・判断力・表現力】

⑨ Vitamin D also **encourages** our body **to** absorb calcium and deactivates **so-called bone-destroying cells**.

◆ encourage ... to ～は「…が～するように促進する［助けとなる］」という意味。
◆ so-called bone-destroying cells は「(1.　　　　　[日本語で]）破骨細胞」という意味。

訳：

⑯ Proper daily meals **are sure to** make your body strong and healthy.

◆ be sure to ～は「(2.　　　　　[日本語で]）～する」という意味。
◆ to-不定詞以下は make＋O＋C の構文。

訳：

Activity Plus 教科書 p.98 ◀意味のまとまりに注意して，本文全体を聞こう。 ◎2-8

①You're starting to think / about improving your eating habits. // ②You have found / some recipes / on the Internet. //

③**Chicken liver in cream** //

④Ingredients / (for 2 people) //　⑤Chicken livers: / 200 g //　⑥Salt: / 1 g //　⑦Pepper: / one pinch //　⑧Onion: / 1/2 //　⑨*Maitake*: / 100 g　⑩Butter: / 8 g //　⑪Sliced garlic: / 1/2 //　⑫Flour: / two teaspoons //　⑬White wine: / one tablespoon //　⑭Milk: / 3/4 cup //　⑮Fresh cream: / 1/4 cup //

⑯Nutrition information / (per person) //

・⑰Energy: / 324 kcal //　・⑱Fat: / 18.6 g //　・⑲Carbohydrate: / 14.7 g //
・⑳Protein: / 23.9 g //　・㉑Vitamin B6: / 0.81 mg //

◇㉒How to cook ◇ //

1. ㉓Cut the chicken livers / into bite-sized pieces / and place them / in salt water. // ㉔Then, / get rid of all the moisture / off the chicken liver pieces / and add the salt and pepper to them. //

2. ㉕Cut an onion / along the fibers / and then / into pieces one centimeter wide. // ㉖Break up a *maitake* mushroom / into pieces. //

3. ㉗Put some butter, / some slices of garlic / and the chicken liver pieces / into a frying pan, / and cook both sides of the liver / on medium heat. //

4. ㉘Add the slices of the onion, / the pieces of *maitake* mushroom / and flour, / and fry them / until the flour completely disappears. //

5. ㉙Add a small amount of white wine / over everything. // ㉚Then, / add milk and fresh cream / when the liquid is gone. // ㉛Finally, / boil on medium heat / until the sauce thickens, / and finish with some salt and pepper. //

㉜**Salmon and spinach gratin** //

㉝Ingredients / (for 2 people) //　㉞Salmon: / 200 g //　㉟Salt: / 2 g //　㊱Onion: / 80 g //　㊲Spinach: / 150 g //　㊳Butter: / 12 g //　㊴*Sake*: / two tablespoons //　㊵Water: / two tablespoons //　㊶Milk: / 1/4 cup //　㊷Ketchup: / one tablespoon //　㊸Cheese: / 30 g //　㊹Nutrition information / (per person) //

・㊺Energy: / 294 kcal //　・㊻Fat: / 12.8 g //　・㊼Carbohydrate: / 10.8 g //
・㊽Calcium: / 235 mg //　・㊾Vitamin D: / 32.2 μg //　・㊿Vitamin K: / 170 μg //

◇51How to cook ◇ //

1. 52Remove the skin / from the salmon, / cut it / into four pieces, / and add some salt and pepper / on top. //

2. 53Cut the onion / into slices. // 54Boil the spinach, / remove the excess moisture / and cut it / into pieces / four or five centimeters long. //

3. 55Fry the onion slices / for one or two minutes / with some butter / in a frying pan. // 56Add the salmon, / *sake* / and water. // 57Cover and fry the salmon / on low heat / for two or three minutes, / then / take the salmon / out of the frying

pan. //

4. ₅₈Add spinach, / milk / and ketchup / to the pan, / and mix them / with 20 grams of the cheese. // ₅₉Move all the ingredients / from the frying pan / to a dish, / and add the salmon / and the remaining 10 grams of cheese / to them. // ₆₀Finally, / bake everything / in an oven / for six to seven minutes / until the cheese is browned. //

📢意味のまとまりに注意して，本文全体を音読しよう。（433 Words）

Words and Phrases	新出単語・表現の意味を調べよう		
liver 名 [lívər] B1	1.	ingredient 名 [ɪngríːdiənt] B1	2.
pepper 名 [pépər] A2	3.	break up …	4.
pinch 名 [píntʃ]	5.	slice 動 [sláɪs] A2	6.
garlic 名 [gáːrlɪk] A2	7.	flour 名 [fláʊər] A2	8.
wine 名 [wáɪn] A2	9.	carbohydrate 名 [kàːrbouháɪdreɪt]	10.
moisture 名 [mɔ́ɪstʃər] B1	11.	frying pan 名 [fráɪŋ pæn] B1	12.
liquid 名 [líkwɪd] B1	13.	boil 動 [bɔ́ɪl] A2	14.
sauce 名 [sɔ́ːs] A2	15.	thicken 動 [θík(ə)n]	16.
salmon 名 [sǽmən] B1	17.	spinach 名 [spínɪtʃ] B1	18.
gratin 名 [grɑ́ːt(ə)n]	19.	ketchup 名 [kétʃəp]	20.
oven 名 [ʌ́v(ə)n] A2	21.	mix A with B	22.

A 【Comprehension】 Answer the following questions in English.

本文のポイントについて答えよう【思考力・判断力・表現力】

1. To get ready to cook the "chicken liver in cream" recipe for four people, how much should the chicken livers weigh?

-----

2. For the "chicken liver in cream" recipe, when should the milk and fresh cream be added?

Paragraphs 1～3

教科書 p.104　　📢意味のまとまりに注意して，本文全体を聞こう。　◎2-10

①"I want to cross over rivers / and the sea." // ②With such a hope / in mind, / people have built / a wide variety of bridges. // ③Do you know / how they are built? // ④What kinds of science are hidden / in them? //

1　⑤The history of bridges is human history. // ⑥Since ancient times, / human beings have flourished / around water. // ⑦They imagined / how crossing over bodies of water / would make travel / much faster. // ⑧The first bridges were simple; / they were made from things / like fallen trees, / making it faster and easier / to connect two places. // ⑨Although stronger materials / such as stone came to be used / in bridge construction, / there were still limitations / on bridge length. // ⑩These limitations led / to new developments. //

2　⑪One example is the stone arch bridge, / used by the Romans / to build the first large, / strong bridges. // ⑫This type of bridge / depended on gravity / holding wedge-shaped stones together. // ⑬Since the stones weighed so much, / the friction between them / was huge / and they wouldn't slide apart. //

3　⑭Another development / was the suspension bridge. // ⑮It was originally made / by combining several vines / and suspending them / from one point to another. // ⑯The first suspension bridges were designed / with the walkway of the bridge / supported by two lines that were fixed / at both ends. // ⑰They had no towers or piers. // ⑱The lines, / which followed a shallow downward arc, / moved in response to loads / on the bridge. //

📢意味のまとまりに注意して，本文全体を音読しよう。(189 Words)

Words and Phrases 新出単語・表現の意味を調べよう			
cross over …	1.	flourish 動 [flə́:rɪʃ]	2.
length 名 [léŋ(k)θ] B1	3.	arch 名 [áːrtʃ] B2	4.
Roman 名 [róumən]	5.	gravity 名 [grǽvəti]	6.
hold … together	7.	wedge 名 [wédʒ]	8.
suspension 名 [səspénʃ(ə)n]	9.	vine 名 [váɪn]	10.
suspend 動 [səspénd] B2	11.	walkway 名 [wɔ́:kwèɪ]	12.
pier 名 [píər]	13.	shallow 形 [ʃǽlou] B1	14.

downward 形 [dáunwərd] B1	15.	arc 名 [áːrk]	16.
load 名 [lóud] A2	17.		

A 【**Comprehension 1**】 Fill in the blanks in Japanese.

要点を整理しよう【思考力・判断力・表現力】

初期の橋：（1.　　　　）な構造（例：倒木，石材）→問題点：橋の（2.　　　　）の限界

新しい
発展

アーチ橋	・くさび形の石を重力が互いに支える ・石は（3.　　　　）によって滑り落ちることがない
吊り橋	・もともとは植物の（4.　　　　）で作っていた ・両端を固定した 2 本の線で支える歩道として設計された ・塔や（5.　　　　）はない

B 【**Comprehension 2**】 Answer the following questions in English.

本文のポイントについて答えよう【思考力・判断力・表現力】

1. What kind of limitations were there in constructing bridges with stone?

2. Who used the stone arch bridge for the first time?

3. How was the suspension bridge originally made?

C 【**Key Sentences**】 Fill in the blanks and translate the following sentences.

重要文について確認しよう【知識・技能】【思考力・判断力・表現力】

⑧ The first bridges were simple; they were made from things like fallen trees, **making it** faster and easier to connect two places.

◆セミコロンは関係のある 2 文をつなぐ。ここでは，後ろの文が前の文の内容を具体的に述べている。

◆ making は付帯状況［同時］を表す分詞構文で，意味上の主語は The first bridges。

◆ it＝（1.　　　　　　　［英語 4 語で］）

訳：

⑬ Since the stones weighed so much, **the friction between them** was huge and they **wouldn't** slide apart.

◆この since は理由を表す接続詞。「…なので」と訳すとよい。

◆ the friction between them とは「（2.　　　　　　［日本語で］）の間に発生する摩擦力」のこと。

◆ wouldn't は「どうしても〜しようとしなかった」の，「意志・拒絶」の意味。

訳：

Paragraphs 4～6

教科書 p.105 ◀意味のまとまりに注意して，本文全体を聞こう。 ◎2-12

4 ①The structures of bridges differ / depending on their length / and purpose. // ②The main components of a bridge / are the foundation, / the substructure, / and the superstructure. // ③Each of them consists of important parts, / and the superstructure determines / the form of the bridge. // ④The three basic bridge forms are / the beam, / the suspension / and the truss. //

5 ⑤Beam bridges are / the most common type of bridge. // ⑥A beam carries vertical loads / by bending. // ⑦Its structure is rather simple / and appropriate / for short bridges. // ⑧Suspension bridges, / which can cover long spans, / carry vertical loads through tension in lines. // ⑨The load is transferred / both to the towers and to the anchorages, / which withstand the inward and vertical pull / of the cables. //

6 ⑩Truss bridges are used / to support great weight. // ⑪They are suitable / for railroad and covered bridges. // ⑫The amount of material / needed to construct them / is small / compared to the weight / they can support. // ⑬A truss is a combination / of many triangles / which makes a stable form, / capable of supporting a considerable external load / over a large span. // ⑭The triangle reduces the stress / caused by any force. // ⑮If a corner of any triangle has a force / on it, / the two sides which make that corner / squeeze together, / and the third side stretches. // ⑯In this way, / triangles divide any force / placed on them. //

◀意味のまとまりに注意して，本文全体を音読しよう。 (217 Words)

Words and Phrases 新出単語・表現の意味を調べよう			
component 名 [kəmpóunənt] B2	1.	substructure 名 [sʌ́bstrʌ̀ktʃər]	2.
superstructure 名 [súːpərstrʌ̀ktʃər]	3.	truss 名 [trʌ́s]	4.
vertical 形 [və́ːrtɪk(ə)l]	5.	be appropriate for …	6.
span 名 [spǽn]	7.	tension 名 [ténʃ(ə)n] B1	8.
transfer 動 [trænsfə́ːr] B1	9.	anchorage 名 [ǽŋk(ə)rɪdʒ] B2	10.
inward 形 [ínwərd]	11.	cable 名 [kéɪb(ə)l] B2	12.

be suitable for …	13.	railroad 名 [réɪlròud] B1	14.
compared to …	15.	capable 形 [kéɪpəb(ə)l] B1	16.
be capable of …	17.	considerable 形 [kənsíd(ə)rəb(ə)l] B1	18.
external 形 [ɪkstə́ːɾn(ə)l] B2	19.	squeeze 動 [skwíːz] B2	20.
stretch 動 [strétʃ] B1	21.		

A 【Comprehension 1】 Fill in the blanks in Japanese.

要点を整理しよう【思考力・判断力・表現力】

橋の構造（橋の構成要素のひとつである（1.　　　　　　　　）が橋の形式を決定する）

ビーム橋 （梁橋）	・曲がることで荷重を伝える ・構造はシンプルで，距離が（2.　　　　　）い橋に向いている
吊り橋	・（3.　　　　　）い距離に架けることができる ・荷重はケーブルを通して塔とアンカレイジに伝わる
トラス橋	・大きな重量に耐えられ，（4.　　　　　　　　）橋や屋根付き橋に適している ・耐荷重と比較して少ない材料で建設できる

└─トラス構造：安定した形である（5.　　　　　　）形を連続的に組み合わせた構造

B 【Comprehension 2】 Answer the following questions in English.

本文のポイントについて答えよう【思考力・判断力・表現力】

1. What determines the form of the bridge?

----

2. Where is the load transferred to in suspension bridges?

----

3. What are truss bridges suitable for?

C 【Key Sentence】 Fill in the blank and translate the following sentence.

重要文について確認しよう【知識・技能】【思考力・判断力・表現力】

⑬ A truss is **a combination of** many triangles which makes a stable form, **capable** of supporting a considerable external load over a large span.

◆a combination of … で「…の（1.　　　　　　[日本語で]）」という意味。

◆文の後半は，形容詞 capable の前に be-動詞の分詞 being が省略されている分詞構文と考える。

訳:--

75

Paragraphs 7〜9　教科書 p.106　🔊意味のまとまりに注意して，本文全体を聞こう。 ⊙2-14

7　①When people choose / which type of bridge to build, / they make decisions / based on the requirements: / the weight of expected traffic, / the environment of the area / and other factors. // ②Bridges are critical parts / of society's infrastructure. // ③Their purpose is / to help people move around safely, / so their structural designs need to be safe. //

8　④Additionally, / bridges have an important role / to play / as local landmarks / in our society. // ⑤The Lucky Knot Bridge / in China / is one of many stunning landmark bridges. // ⑥The design was inspired / by the Möbius strip, / as well as the traditional decorative knot-tying / of Chinese folk art, / where the knot symbolizes / luck and prosperity. // ⑦The Tower Bridge is an attractive landmark / in London. // ⑧It is a huge suspension bridge / that spans the River Thames / and it is also a raisable bridge / which can let large ships through. // ⑨It is known / as an iconic symbol / of London. //

9　⑩In these ways, / bridges are not only important infrastructures / for transportation, / but they also have interesting design aspects. // ⑪Bridges are useful, / and are also pieces of art / and history. // ⑫Bridges help us connect our communities / and bring us closer / together. //

🔊意味のまとまりに注意して，本文全体を音読しよう。（188 Words）

Words and Phrases 新出単語・表現の意味を調べよう			
requirement 名 [rɪkwáɪəʳmənt] B1	1.	critical 形 [krítɪk(ə)l] B1	2.
structural 形 [strʌ́ktʃ(ə)r(ə)l]	3.	additionally 副 [ədíʃ(ə)n(ə)li] B2	4.
landmark 名 [lǽn(d)mὰːʳk]	5.	knot 名 [nɑ́(ː)t] B2	6.
stunning 形 [stʌ́nɪŋ] B1	7.	Möbius strip 名 [mòubiəs stríp]	8.
decorative 形 [dék(ə)rətɪv] B2	9.	prosperity 名 [prɑ(ː)spérəti] B1	10.
Thames [témz]	テムズ川	raisable 形 [réɪzəb(ə)l]	11.

iconic 形 [aɪkɑ́(:)nɪk]	12.	let … through	13.

A 【Comprehension 1】 Fill in the blanks in Japanese.

要点を整理しよう【思考力・判断力・表現力】

地域社会における橋の役割

社会のインフラ	地域の名所
橋の目的は人々が安全に（1.　　　　　） するのに役立つこと ↓ 安全な（2.　　　　　）が求められる	・ラッキー・ノット・ブリッジ（中国） 　―メビウスの帯から着想 　―幸運と（3.　　　　　　）を象徴したデザイン ・タワーブリッジ（ロンドン） 　―巨大な吊り橋，かつ可動橋 　―ロンドンの（4.　　　　　）

B 【Comprehension 2】 Answer the following questions in English.

本文のポイントについて答えよう【思考力・判断力・表現力】

1. What is the purpose of bridges?

2. Why can large ships go through under the Tower Bridge?

3. What do bridges help us do?

C 【Key Sentences】 Fill in the blank and translate the following sentences.

重要文について確認しよう【知識・技能】【思考力・判断力・表現力】

① When people choose **which type of bridge to build**, they make decisions based on the requirements: the weight of expected traffic, the environment of the area and other factors.

   ◆疑問詞＋to-不定詞で名詞のはたらきをする。この which は疑問形容詞で，which type of bridge で名詞句をつくる。which type of bridge to build 全体が choose の目的語。

   ◆コロンの後ろには，（1.　　　　　　　　[英語2語で]）の具体例が列挙されている。

   訳：

⑥ The design was inspired by the Möbius strip, as well as the traditional decorative knot-tying of Chinese folk art, **where** the knot symbolizes luck and prosperity.

   ◆ 関係副詞 where の非制限用法。先行詞は Chinese folk art。

   訳：

Activity Plus 教科書p.110　◀意味のまとまりに注意して，本文全体を聞こう。　⊚2-16

①Suppose / you are a construction worker / in your city. // ②Recently, / three bridges / in the city center / have gotten old. // ③The city wants to improve these bridges. // ④Listen to the request / from the city. //

Location A: ⑤This area is a residential neighborhood / where aesthetics are important, / so high buildings are prohibited. // ⑥Although the span of the new bridge must cover / only 15 meters, / it should be finished / as soon as possible / because many tourists and local people / cross over the river / at this location. // ⑦It will be for pedestrians / only. // ⑧A simple structure with basic support / will be enough. //

Location B: ⑨This bridge is the main hub / to connect to the city center. // ⑩The new bridge will be 300 meters long, / spanning the wide river. // ⑪We want it / to become another landmark / of this city. // ⑫This spot is expected / to have heavy traffic, / so the new bridge must be easy / to maintain. //

Location C: ⑬This bridge is for freight trains / carrying iron ore. // ⑭Due to the extreme heat / last month, / some parts were damaged. // ⑮The new bridge should be strong enough / to endure both heavy loads / and extreme weather conditions. // ⑯It will be 150 meters long. //

◀意味のまとまりに注意して，本文全体を音読しよう。（162 Words）

Words 新出単語の意味を調べよう			
suppose 動 [səpóuz] B1	1.	location 名 [loukéiʃ(ə)n] B1	2.
residential 形 [rèzidénʃ(ə)l] B1	3.	aesthetic 名 [esθétɪk]	4.
pedestrian 名 [pədéstriən] B2	5.	freight 名 [fréɪt]	6.
iron 名 [áɪərn] B1	7.	ore 名 [ɔ́ːr]	8.
extreme 形 [ɪkstríːm] B1	9.	endure 動 [ɪndjúər] B1	10.

【Comprehension 1】 Fill in the blanks in Japanese.

要点を整理しよう【思考力・判断力・表現力】

場所	位置 A	位置 B	位置 C
長さ	15メートル	(3.　　　　) メートル	150メートル
目的	(1.　　　　　　) 専用	交通用	鉄鉱石を運ぶ (5.　　　　) 用
条件	・美観を重視する住宅地のため，高い建物は禁止されている ・橋の使用が多いため，工期は (2.　　　) くする ・シンプルな構造で十分	・都心とつながる中心地である ・街の新たな (4.　　　) にする ・維持管理を容易にする	・重荷と過酷な (6.　　　) 　条件に耐えるようにする

【B】 **【Comprehension 2】** Answer the following questions in English.

本文のポイントについて答えよう【思考力・判断力・表現力】

1. Why are high buildings prohibited in the area for Location A?

....

2. What does the city want the new bridge at Location B to become?

....

【C】 **【Key Sentences】** Fill in the blank and translate the following sentences.

重要文について確認しよう【知識・技能】【思考力・判断力・表現力】

⑤ This area is a residential neighborhood (**where** aesthetics are important), so high buildings are prohibited.

◆関係副詞 where が直前の a residential neighborhood を修飾している。

訳 : ....

⑫ This spot **is expected to** have heavy traffic, so the new bridge must be **easy to maintain**.

◆〈expect＋O＋to～〉で「O が～することを予想する」という意味。ここでは受動態になっている。
◆難易を表す形容詞＋to-不定詞で，「～するには…」という意味を表す。

訳 : ....

⑮ The new bridge should be **strong enough** to endure **both** heavy loads and extreme weather conditions.

◆形容詞＋enough＋to-不定詞で「～するのに十分…」という意味を表す。
◆ both A and B は「A と B の (1.　　　[日本語で])」という意味。

訳 : ....

Paragraphs 1～3

🔊意味のまとまりに注意して，本文全体を聞こう。 💿2-18

①In the United States, / the 1970s were still a time / when discrimination against women could be seen / in daily situations. // ②At that time, / a woman appeared / in court / and devoted her life / to fighting against it. //

1 ③On September 18, 2020, / hundreds of people gathered / in front of the U.S. Supreme Court / for a moment of silence / after the death of one of its justices. // ④Her name was Ruth Bader Ginsburg, / and she was the second female Supreme Court justice / in history. // ⑤She had a strong following / among liberals, / women, / and young people / and was given the nickname / "Notorious RBG." //

2 ⑥Ruth was born / in Brooklyn / in 1933 / to a modest Jewish family. // ⑦When she was a child, / her mother took her / to the library / every week. // ⑧It was natural / for women / to stay home / and not work outside the home / in those days, / but Ruth's mother wanted her daughter / to have a proper education / and become an independent woman. //

3 ⑨In high school, / Ruth was very curious / and tried many things, / including editing the school newspaper, / playing the cello / in an orchestra, / and twirling the baton. // ⑩Her grades were excellent, / and she was chosen / to speak / at her high school graduation. // ⑪However, / she didn't attend the graduation ceremony. // ⑫The day before the ceremony, / her mother, / who had been struggling / with cancer, / had passed away. //

🔊意味のまとまりに注意して，本文全体を音読しよう。(186 Words)

Words and Phrases	新出単語・表現の意味を調べよう		
devote 動 [dɪvóut] B2	1.	devote A to B	2.
supreme 形 [suprí:m]	3.	justice 名 [dʒʌ́stɪs] B1	4.
Ruth Bader Ginsburg [rú:θ béɪdər gínzbɑ:rg]	ルース・ベイダー・ ギンズバーグ	liberal 名 [líb(ə)r(ə)l]	5.
notorious 形 [noutɔ́:riəs] B1	6.	Brooklyn [brʊ́klɪn]	ブルックリン
modest 形 [mɑ́(:)dəst] B2	7.	independent 形 [ìndɪpénd(ə)nt] B1	8.

cello 名 [tʃélou] B2	9.	orchestra 名 [ɔ́:rkɪstrə] B1	10.
twirl 動 [twə́:rl]	11.	baton 名 [bətá(:)n]	12.
graduation 名 [ɡræʤuéɪʃ(ə)n] B1	13.	cancer 名 [kǽnsər] B1	14.
pass away	15.		

A 【Comprehension 1】 Fill in the blanks in Japanese.

要点を整理しよう【思考力・判断力・表現力】

ルース・ベイダー・ギンズバーグ判事（ニックネーム：「ノトーリアス RBG」） ・(1.　　　　　　) として 2 人目の最高裁判所判事	
生誕	・1933年，ブルックリンで（2.　　　　　　　）のユダヤ人家庭に生まれる
子供のとき	・母親に連れられて毎週（3.　　　　　　　）に行く（娘にはきちんとした教育を受けて（4.　　　　　　）した女性になってほしいという母の願い）
高校時代	・(5.　　　　　　) が旺盛で，いろいろなことに挑戦する ・成績優秀で，卒業式でスピーチをすることになる ・式を欠席する　←　前日に母親が（6.　　　　　　）ため

B 【Comprehension 2】 Answer the following questions in English.

本文のポイントについて答えよう【思考力・判断力・表現力】

1. Who was Ruth Bader Ginsburg?

2. What was considered natural for women to do when Ruth was a child?

3. How were Ruth's grades in high school?

C 【Key Sentence】 Fill in the blank and translate the following sentence.

重要文について確認しよう【知識・技能】【思考力・判断力・表現力】

⑫ The day before the ceremony, her mother, (**who had been struggling** with cancer), **had passed away**.

◆この文の主語は（1.　　　　[英語 2 語で]）で，動詞は had passed away の部分にあたる。過去完了形は「過去から見た過去」を表し，卒業式よりさらに以前であることを示している。

◆had been struggling は過去完了進行形で，過去のある時点まで続けられた動作（あるいは，直前まで続いていた動作）を表す。

訳 :

Paragraphs 4〜6

④ ①Ruth entered Cornell University / in 1950 / on a full scholarship. // ②At that time, / the number of female students / attending university / was exceedingly small. // ③Eighty percent of her classmates / were male students. // ④Ruth studied / in secret / because men tended to dislike intelligent women. // ⑤Then / she met Martin Ginsburg, / who was a year ahead of her / in college. // ⑥Unlike many other men, / he liked her intelligence. //

⑤ ⑦After graduating / from Cornell University / in 1954, / Ruth married Martin, / and they had a daughter. // ⑧In 1956, / she entered Harvard Law School, / which her husband was attending. // ⑨She had more than 500 classmates, / and only nine of them / were women. // ⑩There was no ladies' room / in the main building. // ⑪When the building was constructed, / it was not expected / that women would learn law. //

⑥ ⑫In her second year, / unfortunately, / Martin was diagnosed / with cancer. // ⑬Ruth asked his classmates / to take notes / for him / in classes, / and she typed them up / for him every night. // ⑭Without her help, / he could not have graduated. // ⑮She continued to work hard / on her studies / while taking care of her husband / and raising their child. //

📢意味のまとまりに注意して，本文全体を音読しよう。（183 Words）

Words and Phrases 新出単語・表現の意味を調べよう			
Cornell [kɔːrnél]	コーネル	scholarship 名 [skɑ́(:)lərʃip] B1	1.
exceedingly 副 [ɪksíːdɪŋli]	2.	in secret	3.
dislike 動 [dɪsláɪk] A2	4.	intelligent 形 [ɪntélɪdʒ(ə)nt] A2	5.
ahead of ...	6.	unlike 前 [ʌnláɪk] A2	7.
Harvard [hɑ́ːrvərd]	ハーバード	diagnose 動 [dàɪəgnóus]	8.
type ... up	9.		

A 【Comprehension 1】 Fill in the blanks in Japanese.

要点を整理しよう【思考力・判断力・表現力】

大学時代	コーネル大学に在籍：1950年入学，（1.　　　　　）年卒業 ・クラスメートの80パーセントが男子学生 ・男性は（2.　　　　　）が高い女性を嫌う傾向
卒業後	大学時代に出会ったマーティンと結婚して娘をもうける
ロー・スクール時代	ハーバード・ロー・スクールに在籍：1956年入学 ・500人のクラスメートのうち女性はわずか（3.　　　）人 ・本館に女性用の（4.　　　　　）が設置されていない（女性が法律を学ぶことは想定されていなかった） ・（5.　　　　　）と診断された夫を支えながら，自身の勉強や子育てをする

B 【Comprehension 2】 Answer the following questions in English.

本文のポイントについて答えよう【思考力・判断力・表現力】

1. How was Martin different from many other men?

   ....

2. How many female classmates did Ruth have at Harvard Law School?

   ....

3. What happened to Martin when Ruth was in her second year at Harvard Law School?

   ....

C 【Key Sentences】 Fill in the blank and translate the following sentences.

重要文について確認しよう【知識・技能】【思考力・判断力・表現力】

② At that time, **the number of** female students (attending university) **was** exceedingly small.

　◆「…の数」という意味の the number of … は単数扱い。a number of …（多くの…）と区別。

　訳：..

⑧ In 1956, she entered Harvard Law School**, which** her husband was **attending**.

　◆, which の先行詞は Harvard Law School。「…に通う」の意味の attend は他動詞のため, to which としない。

　訳：..

⑭ **Without** her help, he **could not have graduated**.

　◆副詞句 Without her help が仮定法の条件の意味を表している。

　◆ Without her help ＝ If it (1.　　　　　　　　　[英語4語で]) her help

　訳：..

Paragraphs 7〜9

教科書 p.118 ◀意味のまとまりに注意して，本文全体を聞こう。 2-22

7 ①Before she received her degree / at Harvard, / her husband got a job / at a law firm / in New York. // ②The family moved to New York, / and Ruth transferred to Columbia Law School. // ③She graduated / at the top of her class / in 1959 / and looked for a law firm job. // ④However, / no firm would hire her. // ⑤She was female, / had a child, / and was Jewish. //

8 ⑥She never gave up / looking for a job / and began working / as a law clerk / for a district court judge. // ⑦In 1963, / she became a professor / at Rutgers Law School. // ⑧There, / a female professor earned less / than a male professor. // ⑨Ruth, / along with other female faculty members, / sued the school / and won. // ⑩In 1972, / she became the first female tenured professor / at Columbia University. //

9 ⑪Many women / in America / started to speak out / against discrimination against women. // ⑫Ruth co-founded the Women's Rights Project / in 1972 / at the American Civil Liberties Union (ACLU). // ⑬She won five / of six sex-discrimination cases / before the Supreme Court. //

◀意味のまとまりに注意して，本文全体を音読しよう。（166 Words）

Words and Phrases 新出単語・表現の意味を調べよう			
degree 名 [dɪgríː] A2	1.	hire 動 [háɪər] B1	2.
district 名 [dístrɪkt] B1	3.	Rutgers [rʌ́tgərz]	ラトガース
faculty 名 [fǽk(ə)lti] B2	4.	sue 動 [sjúː] B2	5.
tenured 形 [ténjərd]	6.	speak out against …	7.
co-found 動 [kóʊfàʊnd]	8.	liberty 名 [líbərti] A2	9.
sex 名 [séks] B1	10.		

A 【Comprehension 1】 Fill in the blanks in Japanese.

要点を整理しよう【思考力・判断力・表現力】

法律事務員時代	・（1.　　　　　　　）年，編入先のコロンビア・ロー・スクールを卒業する ・法律事務所の就職先を探したが雇ってもらえない 　→女性であること，（2.　　　　　　　）がいること，ユダヤ人であることが理由 ・地方裁判所裁判官のもとで法律事務員の職に就く
大学教授として	・1963年，ラトガース大学ロー・スクールで教授になる ・（3.　　　　　　　）を理由とした給料の格差について訴訟を起こし勝訴する ・1972年，コロンビア大学で（4.　　　　　　　）として最初の終身教授になる
人権運動家として	・1972年，「女性の権利プロジェクト」を共同設立する ・最高裁判所にて6件のうち5件の（5.　　　　　　　）に関する訴訟に勝利する

B 【Comprehension 2】 Answer the following questions in English.

本文のポイントについて答えよう【思考力・判断力・表現力】

1. Why would no firm hire Ruth despite the fact that she graduated at the top of her class?

   ....

2. What was Ruth's first job after she graduated from law school?

   ....

3. In the 1970s, what did many women start to do?

   ....

C 【Key Sentences】 Fill in the blanks and translate the following sentences.

重要文について確認しよう【知識・技能】【思考力・判断力・表現力】

⑨ Ruth, **along with** other female faculty members, sued the school and won.
　◆主語は（1.　　　　　[英語1語で]），動詞は（2.　　　　　[英語1語で]）と（3.　　　　　[英語1語で]）。
　◆ along with ... は「…とともに」という意味。ここでは文中に挿入されている。
　訳：..

⑬ She won **five of six sex-discrimination cases** before **the Supreme Court**.
　◆ five of six sex-discrimination cases で「6つの性差別訴訟のうちの5つ」という意味。
　◆ the Supreme Court は「連邦最高裁判所」のこと。before は court や committee などを目的語とし，「（審議や考慮などのために）…で，…の前に」の意味。
　訳：..

Paragraphs 10〜12

教科書 p.119　◀意味のまとまりに注意して，本文全体を聞こう。　◎2-24

⑩　①Ruth was appointed to the U.S. Court of Appeals / for the District of Columbia / in 1980 / and to the Supreme Court / in 1993. // ②She always went to trial / in support of women's rights, / anti-racism, / and gender equality. // ③Ruth wrote many bitter dissents / to the Supreme Court's majority opinions / while conservative justices had a majority. //

⑪　④Ruth's attitude encouraged young people / who advocated for equal rights / and social justice. // ⑤They started calling Ruth / "Notorious RBG" / after the legendary rapper, / "Notorious B.I.G." // ⑥T-shirts and coffee cups / with her portrait, / miniature figures, / and dolls / became popular. // ⑦Films / based on her life / have been released. // ⑧She was a pop culture icon / as well as a feminist icon. //

⑫　⑨When she was diagnosed / with cancer / in 2009, / Ruth returned to work / only nineteen days / after having surgery. // ⑩When her beloved husband died / in 2010, / she resumed her job / the next day / because that was what he wanted her / to do. // ⑪She continued to fight discrimination / until she died / at the age of 87. // ⑫She was, / as her mother had hoped, / a truly independent woman. //

◀意味のまとまりに注意して，本文全体を音読しよう。（177 Words）

Words and Phrases 新出単語・表現の意味を調べよう			
appoint 動 [əpɔ́ɪnt] B1	1.	appoint A to B	2.
trial 名 [tráɪ(ə)l] B2	3.	in support of …	4.
anti-racism 名 [æ̀ntirèɪsɪz(ə)m]	5.	gender 名 [dʒéndər] A2	6.
equality 名 [ɪkwá(ː)ləti] B1	7.	dissent 名 [dɪsént]	8.
conservative 形 [kənsə́ːrvətɪv] B1	9.	attitude 名 [ǽtətjùːd] A2	10.
rapper 名 [rǽpər]	11.	portrait 名 [pɔ́ːrtrət] A2	12.
miniature 形 [mɪ́niətʃ(ə)r] B2	13.	feminist 名 [fémənɪst]	14.

| surgery 名
[sə́:rdʒ(ə)ri] B1 | 15. | beloved 形
[bɪlʌ́vɪd] B1 | 16. |
| resume 動
[rɪzjúːm] B2 | 17. | | |

A 【Comprehension 1】 Fill in the blanks in Japanese.

要点を整理しよう【思考力・判断力・表現力】

| 最高裁判所
判事として | ・(1.　　　　　)年, 最高裁判所に任命される
・女性の権利, 反人種差別, (2.　　　　　　　)
　を支持する裁判に臨み, 最高裁判所の多
　数意見に対して多くの反対意見を書いた | 若い人々の人権運動を促進
・「ノトーリアス RBG」という
　ニックネーム, グッズ, 映画
　など, (3.　　　　　)のア
　イコンとなる |
| 晩年 | ・がんの（4.　　　　　　　）や夫の死去を経験する中でも精力的に執務にあたる
・(5.　　　　)歳で死去する | |

B 【Comprehension 2】 Answer the following questions in English.

本文のポイントについて答えよう【思考力・判断力・表現力】

1. What happened to Ruth in 1993?

   ----

2. What were the two types of icons that Ruth was considered to be?

   ----

3. Who wanted Ruth to be an independent woman?

C 【Key Sentences】 Fill in the blanks and translate the following sentences.

重要文について確認しよう【知識・技能】【思考力・判断力・表現力】

① Ruth **was appointed to** the U.S. Court of Appeals for the District of Columbia in 1980 |and| **to** the Supreme Court in 1993.

◆ appoint A to B は「A を B に（1.　　　　　[日本語で]）する」という意味。ここでは受動態になっている。

◆接続詞 and は to で始まる 2 つの前置詞句をつないでいる。

訳：----

⑩ When her beloved husband died in 2010, she resumed her job the next day because **that** was [**what** he wanted her to do].

◆ that は「ギンズバーグ判事が自分の仕事を（2.　　　　　[日本語で]）すること」を指す。

◆ what で始まる関係詞節は名詞のはたらきをして, 補語となっている。

訳：----

Activity Plus 教科書 p.124 🔊意味のまとまりに注意して，本文全体を聞こう。◎2-26

①You're looking at an online article / about Ruth Bader Ginsburg's ACLU-era trials. //

②Ruth didn't just insist on women's rights. // ③She believed / all genders should be given equal rights. // ④That belief is reflected / in the trials / she was involved in / as a lawyer. //

⑤In a 1973 Supreme Court case, / for example, / she defended a female lieutenant / who was treated differently / from her male colleagues. // ⑥At the time, / male service members were receiving / housing and medical benefits / for their spouses. // ⑦ However, / when the lieutenant applied for the same benefits, / she was denied them / because she was a woman / and her spouse was a man. // ⑧Federal law stated / that only female service members had to prove / that their husbands depended on them. // ⑨Male service members' wives automatically became dependents. // ⑩The justices, / who were all men, / initially couldn't understand / that this law was discriminatory. // ⑪Ruth convinced them / that treating men and women differently / because of gender / became discrimination. // ⑫As a result, / she won the trial / by a vote of 8-1. //

⑬A trial in 1975 / is also an excellent example / of Ruth's thinking. // ⑭A woman died / during childbirth. // ⑮Her husband decided / to raise their son / and went to the local Social Security office / to ask about parental benefits. // ⑯However, / he learned / that he couldn't apply for the benefit / because he was a man. // ⑰Under the social security law / at that time, / only mothers could get it. // ⑱In the Supreme Court, / Ruth insisted / it was unconstitutional / to withhold benefits / because of gender. // ⑲In the end, / she won the trial. //

⑳In another trial / in 1979, / Ruth pointed out / that the jury selection process involved discrimination. // ㉑At the time, / jury duty was optional / for women / in several states, / while it was compulsory / for men. // ㉒Some women might have been grateful / for the rule / because fulfilling the duty was a burden. // ㉓However, / Ruth argued / that jury duty should be compulsory / for women / as well as men. // ㉔She thought / that women's service / on juries / should be seen to be as valuable / as that of men. //

㉕Through the cases / in which she was involved, / Ruth showed / that there was gender-based discrimination / in the law / and that it hurt everyone. // ㉖She didn't want women / to have special rights. // ㉗She thought / that everyone should be equal / regardless of gender. //

🔊意味のまとまりに注意して，本文全体を音読しよう。(364 Words)

Words and Phrases　新出単語・表現の意味を調べよう

insist 動 [ɪnsíst] B1	1.	insist on …	2.
belief 名 [bɪlíːf] B1	3.	be involved in …	4.
defend 動 [dɪfénd] B1	5.	lieutenant 名 [luːténənt]	6.
spouse 名 [spáʊs]	7.	apply for …	8.
deny 動 [dɪnáɪ] B1	9.	Federal 形 [féd(ə)r(ə)l] B2	10.
initially 副 [ɪníʃ(ə)li] B1	11.	discriminatory 形 [dɪskrímɪnətɔ̀:ri]	12.
childbirth 名 [tʃáɪldbə̀:rθ]	13.	parental 形 [pərént(ə)l] B1	14.
unconstitutional 形 [ʌ̀nkɑ(:)nstətjúːʃ(ə)n(ə)l]	15.	withhold 動 [wɪðhóʊld]	16.
jury 名 [dʒʊ́əri] B2	17.	selection 名 [səlékʃ(ə)n] B1	18.
optional 形 [ɑ́(:)pʃ(ə)nəl] B2	19.	compulsory 形 [kəmpʌ́ls(ə)ri] B2	20.
fulfill 動 [fʊlfíl] B2	21.	burden 名 [bə́:rd(ə)n] B1	22.
regardless 副 [rɪɡɑ́:rdləs] B2	23.	regardless of …	24.

A 【Comprehension】 Fill in the blanks in Japanese.

要点を整理しよう【思考力・判断力・表現力】

訴訟	概要		主張
1973年	女性中尉が男性の配偶者に対する手当を申請したが拒否された。連邦法によると，女性軍人は夫が妻に頼っていることを（1.　　　　）しなければならなかった。	←	性別を理由に男女の扱いが異なることは（2.　　　　）となるのではないか。
1975年	妻を亡くした男性が手当を（3.　　　　）することができなかった。当時の社会保障法によると，母親だけが手当を受け取ることができた。	←	性別を理由に手当を支給しないことは（4.　　　　）に反するのではないか。
1979年	いくつかの州において，女性は陪審員の職務が（5.　　　　）ではなかった。陪審員の職務は（6.　　　　）だったため，このルールを歓迎する女性もいたとみられる。	←	女性の陪審員としての活動は男性と同様の（7.　　　　）としてみなされるべきではないか。

Paragraphs 1～3

教科書 p.130　◀意味のまとまりに注意して，本文全体を聞こう。 2-28

①Tatsuya Miyo was involved / in a car accident / at the age of eighteen. // ②At that time, / as a teenager, / he often wondered, / "What is the meaning / of my life?" //

☐1　③I found myself / lying on a bed. // ④According to the doctor, / I suffered a cervical spinal cord injury / when I collided head-on with a car / on my motorbike. // ⑤After a few months / of rehabilitation, / I thought, / "If I have to stay / in a wheelchair / for the rest of my life, / it will be over." //

☐2　⑥After moving from hospital to hospital, / I finally entered / a rehabilitation facility / in Shizuoka Prefecture. // ⑦There, / I met a middle-aged man / who had the same disability. // ⑧He gave me precious advice, / and I started / to think of him / as my mentor. // ⑨Thanks to his advice, / I gradually came to feel positive / about my situation. //

☐3　⑩When I was wondering / about how to live my life, / fond memories of traveling / came to mind. // ⑪I had an idea / to plan a trip / that could help others / who are in a similar difficult situation / to mine. // ⑫Since I first went abroad / to Hawaii / at the age of 23, / my outlook on life / had changed dramatically. // ⑬In the summer / when I was 28, / I set off / on a nine-month journey / around the world / by myself, / sharing my travel experiences / in a wheelchair / as well as overseas barrier-free information. //

◀意味のまとまりに注意して，本文全体を音読しよう。（197 Words）

Words and Phrases 新出単語・表現の意味を調べよう			
teenager 名 [tíːnèɪdʒər] A2	1.	cervical 形 [sáːrvɪk(ə)l]	2.
collide 動 [kəláɪd]	3.	collide with …	4.
motorbike 名 [móʊtərbàɪk] B2	5.	rehabilitation 名 [rìːəbɪlɪtéɪʃ(ə)n]	6.
facility 名 [fəsíləti] B1	7.	disability 名 [dìsəbíləti] B1	8.
precious 形 [préʃəs] B1	9.	mentor 名 [méntɔːr] B2	10.
wonder about …	11.	fond 形 [fá(ː)nd] B1	12.

| outlook 名
[áʊtlùk] B2 | 13. | dramatically 副
[drəmǽtɪk(ə)li] B2 | 14. |
| journey 名
[dʒə́ːrni] A2 | 15. | barrier-free 形
[bæ̀riərfríː] B1 | 16. |

A 【Comprehension 1】 Fill in the blanks in Japanese.

要点を整理しよう【思考力・判断力・表現力】

三代達也さんが旅に出るまでの経緯

- ・18歳のときに交通事故で頚髄損傷を負い，その後，車いすで（1.　　　　　）生活を送る
- ・自分と同じ障害のある中年の男性に出会う
  ‖
  三代さんにとっての「（3.　　　　　）」

「（2.　　　　　）生活を残りの人生で続けなければならないのなら終わりだ。」

自分の状況について，徐々に（4.　　　　　）に感じるようになる

- ・自分と同じような困難な状況にある人々を助ける旅行を計画しようと思いつく
  →ハワイに行く（23歳）→（5.　　　　　）で９か月の車いす世界一周の旅に出発する（28歳）

B 【Comprehension 2】 Answer the following questions in English.

本文のポイントについて答えよう【思考力・判断力・表現力】

1. How did Tatsuya think his life would be if he had to stay in a wheelchair for the rest of it?

2. What did Tatsuya start to think of the middle-aged man as?

3. What did Tatsuya share during his journey around the world?

C 【Key Sentences】 Fill in the blank and translate the following sentences.

重要文について確認しよう【知識・技能】【思考力・判断力・表現力】

③ I **found** myself lying on a bed.
   ◆ find oneself ～ing で，「自分が～していることに気づく」という意味。
   訳：

⑪ I had an idea to plan a trip (**that** could help others (**who** are in a similar difficult situation to **mine**)).
   ◆２か所の関係代名詞節が，直前にある a trip と others をそれぞれ修飾している。
   ◆ mine＝my（1.　　　[英語１語で]）
   訳：

Paragraphs
4～6

教科書 p.131　🔊意味のまとまりに注意して，本文全体を聞こう。 2-30

4　①Soon after I set out, / a scam group stole 50,000 yen / from me / at the Louvre Museum / in Paris. // ②When I returned to my hotel / in shock, / I talked with a clerk, / whom later I nicknamed Pierre. // ③"I'm shocked. // ④I'll hate Paris / because of the trouble / at the Louvre." // ⑤He listened to me carefully / and gave me / his contact information. //

5　⑥The next morning, / I got an email / from Pierre: / "We decided / to serve you breakfast / for free." // ⑦I almost cried / and thankfully replied, / "Why don't we go / for dinner?" // ⑧Then / I got an unexpected message: / "Let's go / to the Louvre / again." // ⑨I was reluctant to go, / but I really enjoyed the museum / with Pierre's humorous explanation. // ⑩After leaving there / in the evening, / Pierre looked up / at the night sky / and said, / "I wanted to change your sad Louvre / into a memorable one." // ⑪His words shook my heart. //

6　⑫The incident / at the Louvre / certainly made me feel negatively / about Paris, / but thanks to Pierre, / I left Paris / with good memories. // ⑬Even if you face something / you don't like, / you may still get a good impression / about it / afterwards / as long as you don't stick to the first impression. // ⑭What I learned from Pierre / had a great influence / on my way of thinking. //

🔊意味のまとまりに注意して，本文全体を音読しよう。(211 Words)

Words and Phrases	新出単語・表現の意味を調べよう		
scam 名 [skǽm]	1.	in shock	2.
Pierre [pjéər]	ピエール	thankfully 副 [θǽŋkf(ə)li]	3.
unexpected 形 [ʌ̀nɪkspéktɪd] B1	4.	humorous 形 [hjú:m(ə)rəs] B1	5.
explanation 名 [èksplənéɪʃ(ə)n] A2	6.	memorable 形 [mém(ə)rəb(ə)l] B1	7.
negatively 副 [négətɪvli] B2	8.	as long as …	9.

A 【Comprehension 1】 Fill in the blanks in Japanese.

要点を整理しよう【思考力・判断力・表現力】

パリでの経験

・ルーブル美術館で（1.　　　　　　　　）を盗まれる ・ホテルに戻り，そのことをフロント係のピエールに話す	「ルーブルでのトラブルで，パリが（2.　　　　　　　）になりそうだ。」
・ピエールにルーブルの再訪を誘われ，ピエールの（3.　　　　　　　）のある説明で楽しむ	「悲しい経験をしたルーブルを，（4.　　　　　　　）ルーブルに変えたかった」	よい思い出とともにパリを出発する

→「（5.　　　　　　　）にこだわらなければ，後でよい印象を得ることがあるかもしれない」

B 【Comprehension 2】 Answer the following questions in English.

本文のポイントについて答えよう【思考力・判断力・表現力】

1. What was Pierre's job?

2. What was the second visit to the Louvre Museum like for Tatsuya?

3. According to Tatsuya, what should we do if we face something we don't like?

C 【Key Sentences】 Translate the following sentences.

重要文について確認しよう【知識・技能】【思考力・判断力・表現力】

② When I returned to my hotel in shock, I talked with <u>a clerk</u>, (**whom** later <u>I</u> <u>nicknamed</u> <u>Pierre</u>).

◆目的格の関係代名詞 whom の非制限用法。直前の a clerk を補足的に説明している。動詞 nickname が S＋V＋O＋C の文型を作っており，O が関係代名詞として前に出ている。

訳：

⑫ The incident (at the Louvre) certainly **made** me **feel** negatively about Paris, but thanks to Pierre, I left Paris with good memories.

◆ at で始まる形容詞句が直前の the incident を修飾している。

◆ make は使役動詞。make＋O＋〜で「O に〜させる」という意味。

訳：

Paragraphs 7~9

教科書 p.132 ◀意味のまとまりに注意して，本文全体を聞こう。 ◉ 2-32

7 ①When I traveled / to Athens, / Greece, / I met a man / who had come from India. // ②During my visit / to the Parthenon, / he kindly gave me support, / which was beyond my expectation. // ③When I asked the man / what made him so kind, / he replied, / "We were all born / and grew up / in this universe. // ④Gender, / age, / and disability / don't matter / at all. // ⑤I just had time / today / to help you. // ⑥Thank you / for giving me / such a wonderful day." //

8 ⑦On hearing his words, / I realized / it was incorrect / to assume / that others would mind helping me / with my disability. // ⑧Before I started traveling, / I felt / it was sad and inconvenient / to be confined / to a wheelchair. // ⑨What I learned / during my travel / to Athens / was very simple: / I can stay / just the way I am. //

9 ⑩Now, / I want to create an environment / where everyone can enjoy traveling. // ⑪If your life is boring / with daily routines, / traveling will give you a departure / from your normal life. // ⑫Take a step / forward / and experience something unusual / by making changes / yourself. // ⑬If you do that, / I believe / you can grow / by thinking about your life, / relying on others / and studying by yourself. //

◀意味のまとまりに注意して，本文全体を音読しよう。(197 Words)

Words and Phrases	新出単語・表現の意味を調べよう		
Athens [ǽθɪnz]	アテネ	Greece [gríːs]	1.
Parthenon [páːrθənà(ː)n]	パルテノン	expectation 名 [èkspektéɪʃ(ə)n] B2	2.
beyond (one's) expectation	3.	on ~ing	4.
incorrect 形 [ìnkərékt] B1	5.	assume 動 [əsjúːm] B1	6.
inconvenient 形 [ìnkənvíːniənt] B1	7.	confine 動 [kənfáɪn] B2	8.
routine 名 [ruːtíːn] B1	9.	departure 名 [dɪpáːrtʃər] B1	10.
rely 動 [rɪláɪ] B1	11.	rely on …	12.

A 【Comprehension 1】 Fill in the blanks in Japanese.

要点を整理しよう【思考力・判断力・表現力】

ギリシャでの経験

- アテネのパルテノン神殿で（1.　　　　　　）か
  ら来た男性がとても親切にサポートしてくれた

  私たちはみなこの宇宙に生まれて成長した。
  性別，年齢，（2.　　　　　　）はまったく関
  係ない。

「車いすに拘束されるのは（3.　　　　　　）
て（4.　　　　　　）なことだ」

「自分はありのままの自分でいることができ
る」

三代さんの今の願い：「だれもが（5.　　　　　　）を楽しむことができる環境を作りたい」

B 【Comprehension 2】 Answer the following questions in English.

本文のポイントについて答えよう【思考力・判断力・表現力】

1. What did Tatsuya ask the man from India?

2. What did Tatsuya learn during his travel to Athens?

3. According to Tatsuya, what will give you a departure from your normal life
   and daily routines?

C 【Key Sentences】 Fill in the blanks and translate the following sentences.

重要文について確認しよう【知識・技能】【思考力・判断力・表現力】

② During my visit to the Parthenon, he kindly gave me support, which was
beyond my expectation.

◆ beyond my expectation は「私が期待していなかったような，期待した以上の」という意味。

訳：

⑦ **On hearing** his words, I realized it was incorrect to assume that others would
mind helping me with my disability.

◆ on 〜ing で「〜すると（1.　　　　[日本語で]）」という意味。
◆ mind 〜ing で「〜するのをいやがる」という意味。

訳：

⑬ If you do **that**, I believe you can grow by thinking about your life, relying on
others and studying by yourself.

◆ that の具体的な内容は，「一歩踏み出して，いつもと（2.　　　　[日本語で]）ことを体験すること」。

訳：

Paragraphs 10〜12

教科書 p.133 ◁意味のまとまりに注意して，本文全体を聞こう。 2-34

⑩ ①After suffering my injury, / I sometimes wanted to die, / but now / I'm glad / I am alive. // ②When you feel like isolating yourself / from society, / it's a great adventure / for you / to step outside. // ③Traveling is a life textbook / with no printed pages. // ④The content of the textbook is different, / depending on your stage / in life, / and is always changing. //

⑪ ⑤I cherished three ideas / I had learned / from my mentor / ── encounter, / challenge / and action. // ⑥Meet someone / and discover a new sense of values / that you hadn't noticed / on your own. // ⑦By taking on challenges, / you accumulate small successful experiences / and gain confidence. // ⑧The experience / gained through encounters / and the confidence / cultivated through repeated challenges / will broaden the range of your actions / in the world. //

⑫ ⑨A friend of mine / in Hawaii / gave me a wonderful phrase: / "No Rain, / No Rainbow." // ⑩Anyone can feel down / when it rains. // ⑪However, / don't forget / that the rain is necessary / for you / to fully enjoy the rainbow / of happiness / that follows. // ⑫I believe / bad things will often change / into better things / afterwards. // ⑬If something unpleasant happens, / you can think / "That was a necessary rain" / in the end. //

◁意味のまとまりに注意して，本文全体を音読しよう。（191 Words）

Words and Phrases 新出単語・表現の意味を調べよう			
isolate 動 [áɪsəlèɪt]	1.	isolate A from B	2.
take on …	3.	encounter 名 [ɪnkáʊntər] B1	4.
accumulate 動 [əkjúːmjəlèɪt] B2	5.	confidence 名 [ká(:)nfɪd(ə)ns] B1	6.
cultivate 動 [kʌ́ltɪvèɪt] B1	7.	unpleasant 形 [ʌnpléz(ə)nt] A2	8.

A 【Comprehension 1】 Fill in the blanks in Japanese.

要点を整理しよう【思考力・判断力・表現力】

三代さんが大事にしている考え方

旅をすること ＝「(1.　　　　　) されたページのない教科書」
└内容は人生のステージによって異なり，常に (2.　　　　　) する

出会い：自分では気づかなかった新しい
(3.　　　　　) を発見する

挑戦：小さな成功経験を蓄積して，
(4.　　　　　) を得る

行動：出会いで得た経験と繰り返し挑戦することで育てた自信が，世界で行動できる
(5.　　　　　) を広げる

「No Rain, No Rainbow」（ハワイの友人が教えてくれた言葉）
→幸せの (6.　　) を楽しむには (7.　　) が必要。悪いことは後でよいことに変わることもある

B 【Comprehension 2】 Answer the following questions in English.

本文のポイントについて答えよう【思考力・判断力・表現力】

1. What does Tatsuya compare traveling to?

2. According to Tatsuya, how do we accumulate small successful experiences and gain confidence?

3. What does Tatsuya believe bad things will change into afterwards?

C 【Key Sentences】 Fill in the blanks and translate the following sentences.

重要文について確認しよう【知識・技能】【思考力・判断力・表現力】

④ The content of the textbook is different, **depending** on your stage in life, and is always changing.

◆ depend on ... は「… (1.　　　　　) だ」という意味。depending on は分詞構文の形だが，前置詞のように扱われる。

訳：

⑧ The experience (**gained** through encounters) and the confidence (**cultivated** through repeated challenges) will **broaden** the range of your actions in the world.

◆過去分詞 gained と cultivated が，直前の名詞をそれぞれ修飾している。
◆この文の動詞は broaden である。「…を (2.　　　　　)」という意味。

訳：

97

Activity Plus 教科書 p.138 🔊意味のまとまりに注意して，本文全体を聞こう。 ◎2-36

①You found an interview article / about Yui Kamiji / on the Internet. //

②Yui Kamiji started wheelchair tennis / at the age of 11 / and was ranked No.1 / in Japan / at the age of 14. // ③She played / in the London 2012 Paralympic Games / in her third year / of high school / and was finally ranked No.1 / in the world / in 2014. // ④In the Tokyo 2020 Paralympics, / she won / the silver medal. // ⑤Let's learn / about her story. //

■⑥Interview // ⑦I was originally able to walk / with orthoses, / but as I grew up, / it became harder / for me / to walk. // ⑧Despite facing difficulties / ever since I was a child, / if I was going to do something, / I wanted to do it / under the same conditions / as everyone else. // ⑨For example, / when I was in elementary school, / my teacher said / that I could not take part / in a relay race / because I might trip / and hurt myself / if I ran. // ⑩This really annoyed me. // ⑪I thought / it should be the same / for everyone. // ⑫Why was I the only one / who could not take part / in the race? //

⑬Since I was very young, / my parents / and others close to me / created an environment / where I could try anything / I wanted to do. // ⑭They respected my wishes. // ⑮I am very grateful for that. // ⑯I learned the importance / of clearly conveying to others / what I wanted to do / and what I could do / myself, / and also / of asking others / for their help and cooperation / when necessary. // ⑰I also learned / the importance / of understanding how many people had helped me / to get to where I am, / and of feeling gratitude / toward them. // ⑱These ideas became an important part / of my identity. // ⑲It is about / how I should be / as a person, / which comes before / how I should be / as an athlete, / and I think of that / every day. //

🔊意味のまとまりに注意して，本文全体を音読しよう。(295 Words)

Words and Phrases 新出単語・表現の意味を調べよう			
orthoses 名 [ɔːrθóʊsiːz] < orthosis 名 [ɔːrθóʊsɪs]	1.	annoy 動 [ənɔ́ɪ] A2	2.
close to …	3.	convey 動 [kənvéɪ] B1	4.
cooperation 名 [koʊɑ̀(ː)pəréɪʃ(ə)n] B2	5.		

A 【Comprehension 1】 Fill in the blanks in Japanese.

要点を整理しよう【思考力・判断力・表現力】

上地結衣選手（車いすテニス）のインタビュー

経験	・成長するにつれて（1.　　　　　　　）のが困難になった ・何かしようとするときに，みんなと同じ（2.　　　　　　）のもとでしたいと思っていた ・両親や身近な人が何でも挑戦できる（3.　　　　　）を作ってくれた
学んだこと	・自分がしたいこととできることを人にはっきり（4.　　　　　　）ことの重要性 ・必要なとき，人に助けや（5.　　　　　）を求めることの重要性 ・今いる場所にたどり着くのに多くの人が助けてくれたことを理解することの重要性 ・その人たちに（6.　　　　　）することの重要性

└─自分のアイデンティティの重要な部分：「何よりも（7.　　　　　）としてどうあるべきか」

B 【Comprehension 2】 Answer the following questions in English.

本文のポイントについて答えよう【思考力・判断力・表現力】

1. What was Yui's achievement in the Tokyo 2020 Paralympics?

　　...

2. Why did the teacher say Yui could not take part in the relay race?

　　...

3. What is Yui grateful for?

　　...

C 【Key Sentences】 Fill in the blanks and translate the following sentences.

重要文について確認しよう【知識・技能】【思考力・判断力・表現力】

⑩ **This** really **annoyed** me.

　◆ This は「(1.　　　　　　　　　　　[日本語で])」こと。

　◆無生物主語のため，自然な意味になるように工夫して訳す。

　訳:...

⑫ Why was I the only one (**who** could not **take part in** the race)?

　◆ who で始まる関係代名詞節が直前の one を修飾している。one は「人」という意味。

　◆ take part in ... は「…に（2.　　　　　　）する」という意味。

　訳:...

⑯ I learned the importance of [clearly **conveying to** others what I wanted to do and what I could do myself], and also of [asking others for their help and cooperation when necessary].

　◆ the importance of ... の of で始まる前置詞句が2つ続く。

　◆ convey A to B で「A を B に伝える」。A が長いので，to B (to others) を先に示している。

　訳:...

Part 1 教科書 p.144 ◀意味のまとまりに注意して，本文全体を聞こう。 ◉2-38

①WANTED // ②University student / to sit / with elderly woman // ③between 3 and 6 p.m., // ④Monday through Friday //

⑤Peter Brent needed money / and was ready / to do any kind of work. // ⑥When he read the newspaper advertisement / he decided / he could even sit / three hours a day / with an elderly woman / if necessary. //

⑦Peter rang the bell. // ⑧In a few seconds / a young woman / in a black uniform / opened the door. //

⑨"I've come about the advertisement," / Peter told her. // ⑩The young woman looked at him / rather strangely. // ⑪"I'll tell Ms. Marvin," / she said, / and disappeared. //

⑫A moment later / a woman / in her late thirties / appeared. // ⑬"There must be some mistake," / she said. //

⑭"It's about your advertisement / in the newspaper," / Peter explained. //

⑮"Yes, / I know, / but you see, / we wanted a woman / for the position, / not a man." //

⑯"The notice simply said / 'university student.'" //

⑰"I'm terribly sorry, / but we really need a woman / to care for my mother." //

⑱At that moment / a woman in a wheelchair / entered from another room. // ⑲She seemed quite old / but sat in her chair / with great dignity, / rather like a queen. // ⑳"Who is this, / Celia?" / she asked, / pointing at Peter. //

㉑"He's come about the position / we discussed, / Mother, / someone / to stay with you / when I'm out." //

㉒"I've told you / a hundred times, / Celia, / I'm not a baby! // ㉓I don't need to be sat with." //

㉔"Mother, / we've talked that / all over. // ㉕You can't be here / alone / for three hours / every afternoon. // ㉖The servants are busy / and ...." //

㉗"And you have to play cards / and talk with your friends!" //

㉘"Mother!" //

㉙"Well, / it's true." //

㉚"I've just told the young man / we want a woman / for this position." //

㉛"Why? // ㉜Listen to me, / Celia. // ㉝I'm the one / to decide / who is going to stay with me / —— if anyone is." //

㉞"I really think, / Mother ...." //

◀意味のまとまりに注意して，本文全体を音読しよう。（302 Words）

Words and Phrases 新出単語・表現の意味を調べよう

Peter Brent [píːtər brént]	ピーター・ブレント	if necessary	1.

Marvin [mɑ́ːrvɪn]	マーヴィン	care for …	2.
dignity 名 [díɡnəti] B2	3.	Celia [síːljə]	シーリア
all over	4.		

A 【Comprehension 1】 Fill in the blanks in Japanese.

要点を整理しよう【思考力・判断力・表現力】

ピーターは，平日の午後に高齢の女性の世話をする（1.　　　　　）を募集する新聞広告を見つける。 ➡ ピーターは新聞広告を出した家に行き，新聞広告のことで来たことを伝える。 ➡ （2.　　　）歳代後半のシーリアという女性が現れ，募集しているのは（3.　　　　）であることを伝える。 ➡

➡ （4.　　　　　）に乗った高齢の女性（シーリアの（5.　　　　）がやって来て，ピーターに気づく。 ➡ ピーターの前で二人が口論をする。高齢の女性の主張は，「自分の世話をする人は必要ない。もしだれかが自分といっしょにいるというのであれば，だれにするかを決めるのは（6.　　　　　　）だ」という内容。

B 【Comprehension 2】 Answer the following questions in English.

本文のポイントについて答えよう【思考力・判断力・表現力】

1.　What was wrong with Peter Brent answering the advertisement?

2.　Who was Celia to the elderly woman?

C 【Key Sentences】 Fill in the blanks and translate the following sentences.

重要文について確認しよう【知識・技能】【思考力・判断力・表現力】

① WANTED / University student to sit with elderly woman / between 3 and 6 p.m., / Monday through Friday

　◆限られたスペースで表現するために一部の語が省略されている。（1.　　[英語1語で]）university student to sit with （2.　　[英語1語で]）elderly woman between 3 and 6 p.m., Monday through Friday, （3.　　[英語1語で]）wanted.

　訳 :---

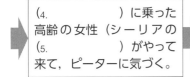

㉝ I'm the one (**to decide** who is going to stay with me) ── if anyone is.

　◆ to-不定詞句は形容詞用法。直前の the one を修飾している。

　◆ if anyone is は後ろに going to stay with me が省略されている。

　訳 :---

Part 2 教科書 p.146 ◁意味のまとまりに注意して，本文全体を聞こう。 ◉2-40

①"All right! // ②If you insist / that I have a sitter / I'll take him!" // ③She pointed at Peter / again. // ④"After all, / it's my money / that's going to be paid, / so I decide / who's going to be here. // ⑤What's your name, / young man?" //

⑥"Peter Brent." //

⑦"Well, / Peter, / if you're going to work / here, / why not start / now? // ⑧Come along! // ⑨Push me / into the next room. // ⑩We'll discuss / what you have to do / in private." // ⑪Peter looked at Ms. Marvin / but she only looked back / as if to say / "What can I do?" //

⑫So / Peter took the job / ── rather, / the job took Peter! // ⑬Five minutes after being told / he wouldn't do / he found himself working. //

⑭"I forgot / to introduce myself. // ⑮I am Ms. Arthur Carlyle," / she said / "and this room is my little world." //

⑯She began / to tell Peter / about herself, / and there was much / to tell / ── about her dead husband, / her three children, / now all married, / and her life / until now. // ⑰Peter decided / he was going to like Ms. Carlyle, / although at the same time / he was just a bit afraid of her, / too. //

⑱"So, / young man, / you know all / about me," / she said, / "and what about you? // ⑲If you're going to be here / three hours / every day / there are things / for me / to know about you, / too." //

⑳Peter gave Ms. Carlyle a short history of / himself. // ㉑"I'm in my last year / of university," / he finished, / "studying English Literature. // ㉒I want to be a teacher." //

㉓"You won't get rich, / but that isn't important, / you know. // ㉔Arthur and I were happiest / when we had nothing / but each other." // ㉕Ms. Carlyle smiled / for the first time. // ㉖"I like you, / Peter Brent, / but then I knew / immediately I was going to." //

㉗"I'm glad, / but how did you know?" //

◁意味のまとまりに注意して，本文全体を音読しよう。（295 Words）

Words and Phrases 新出単語・表現の意味を調べよう			
sitter 名 [sítər]	1.	after all	2.
why not …?	3.	in private	4.
Arthur Carlyle [á:rθər ka:rláil]	アーサー・カーライル	at the same time	5.

A 【Comprehension 1】 Fill in the blanks in Japanese.

要点を整理しよう【思考力・判断力・表現力】

高齢の女性（カーライルさん）はピーターを雇うことに決める。	カーライルさんはピーターを自分の部屋に連れて行き，自己紹介をする。亡き夫，(1.) 人の子供，これまでの自分の (2.) のことについて話す。	ピーターはカーライルさんのことを好きになりそうな一方で，同時に少し (3.) の気持ちも持つ。

カーライルさんはピーターに自己紹介をするように促す。	ピーターは自己紹介をする。大学の最終学年にいて (4.) を学んでおり，(5.) を目指していることを話す。	カーライルさんは夫との幸せな時を思い出し，初めて (6.) を見せる。そして，ピーターのことを気に入っていることを伝える。

B 【Comprehension 2】 Answer the following questions in English.

本文のポイントについて答えよう【思考力・判断力・表現力】

1. What did Ms. Carlyle want to do with Peter in the next room?

2. How did Ms. Carlyle describe her own room?

3. What did Peter study at his university?

C 【Key Sentences】 Fill in the blanks and translate the following sentences.

重要文について確認しよう【知識・技能】【思考力・判断力・表現力】

⑪ Peter looked at Ms. Marvin but she only looked back **as if to say** "What can I do?"

◆ as if to say ... は「まるで…と言わんばかりに」という意味。

訳：

⑬ Five minutes after being told he wouldn't **do** he **found** himself working.

◆この do は具体的には (1.   [英語1語で]) the job のこと。

◆ find＋O＋～ing で「O が～しているのに気づく」という意味。

訳：

㉔ Arthur and I were **happiest** when we had **nothing but** each other.

◆比べているのがその人たち自身についてのことなので，最上級 happiest には the をつけない。

◆ nothing but ... は「… (2.   [日本語で])」という意味。

訳：

Part 3　教科書 p.148　📢意味のまとまりに注意して，本文全体を聞こう。　◎2-42

①"I'm an old woman. // ②I've lived many years / and met many people, / good and bad. // ③A young man / who will sit / with a dull, / demanding old woman / day after day / because he wants money / to study / and become a teacher / has to have some good / in him. // ④Also …" / her voice suddenly turned soft, / "you remind me / of my Arthur. // ⑤He looked very much like you / when I married him." //

⑥"Now, / what is it / you're to do / when you come?" / she asked / finally. //

⑦"I have no idea. // ⑧Ms. Marvin didn't tell me." //

⑨The old lady laughed. // ⑩"I didn't give her time. // ⑪Well, / we have plans to make / then / and we'll make them / as we wish. // ⑫I suppose, / Peter, / you had some idea / of sitting here / every day / and studying / while I slept / in my chair. // ⑬Right?" //

⑭"Well, I …." //

⑮"Wrong! // ⑯Why should you sit here / with the writing of Shakespeare, / Thackeray / and Dickens / to enjoy all by yourself / day after day / and not share them / with me? // ⑰I've never had a chance / to study them, / but as they say, / you're never too old / to learn." //

⑱"You mean / you want me to read / to you?" //

⑲"No, / Peter. // ⑳That takes too long. // ㉑I've still got good eyes / and can read. // ㉒Tell me / what you're working on; / I'll read it / in the morning / and we can talk about it / in the afternoon. // ㉓How does that seem?" //

㉔"Fine." // ㉕What else was there / to say / but "Fine"? // ㉖After all, / he was going to be paid / to come here / every day. // ㉗He had some doubts, / however. // ㉘What use was it going to be / to discuss English Literature / with an old woman / in a wheelchair? //

㉙"Where do we begin?" / asked Ms. Carlyle, / her eyes already bright / with excitement. //

㉚"Well, / for our next class / we will compare the characters / of King Lear and Hamlet. // ㉛Whose life was more tragic?" //

📢意味のまとまりに注意して，本文全体を音読しよう。（311 Words）

Words and Phrases	新出単語・表現の意味を調べよう		
dull 形 [dʌ́l] B1	1.	day after day	2.
Shakespeare [ʃéɪkspɪər]	シェークスピア	Thackeray [θǽk(ə)ri]	サッカレー
Dickens [díkɪnz]	ディケンズ	excitement 名 [ɪksáɪtmənt] B1	3.

Lear [líər]	リア王	Hamlet [hǽmlət]	ハムレット
tragic 形 [trǽdʒɪk] B1	4.		

 【Comprehension 1】 Fill in the blanks in Japanese.

要点を整理しよう【思考力・判断力・表現力】

カーライルさんは，ピーターが（1.　　）に似ていることを伝える。 → カーライルさんは，ピーターの仕事に関して，自分たちが（2.　　）ように計画を立てようと提案する。 → カーライルさんは，それまで英文学を読む（3.　　）がなく，今からでも（4.　　）意志があることをピーターに話す。 →

→ カーライルさんは，午前に読んだ英文学について，（5.　　）に二人で話をするという方法を提案する。 → ピーターは同意するものの，このことが何の役に立つのか少しの（6.　　）を感じる。 → カーライルさんは英文学を読むことを楽しみにする。ピーターは次回に話し合うテーマを予告する。

B **【Comprehension 2】** Answer the following questions in English.

本文のポイントについて答えよう【思考力・判断力・表現力】

1. What proverb did Ms. Carlyle mention?

2. Why didn't Ms. Carlyle think it was a good idea for Peter to read to her?

C **【Key Sentences】** Fill in the blanks and translate the following sentences.

重要文について確認しよう【知識・技能】【思考力・判断力・表現力】

⑥ "Now, **what** is it **you're to do** when you come?" she asked finally.

◆ what is you're to do? が強調構文となっている。強調された what が文頭に出て，その後は疑問文の語順。
◆ be-動詞に to-不定詞を続けると，「〜する予定になっている」などの意味を表すことができる。
訳:

⑯ Why should you [**sit** here with the writing of Shakespeare, Thackeray and Dickens to enjoy all by yourself day after day] and [**not share them** with me]?

◆接続詞 and が，sit で始まる動詞句と not share で始まる動詞句をつないでいる。
◆ them＝（1.　　　　　　　　　　　　　[英語4語で]）
訳:

105

Part 4 教科書 p.150 📢意味のまとまりに注意して，本文全体を聞こう。 ◎2-44

①"That's rather a big order / to fill, / Peter. // ②I've seen both plays / but many years ago. // ③I'll have to read / this evening / and tomorrow morning, / too. // ④I'm sure / we have a volume of Shakespeare / in the house / somewhere. // ⑤Well, / you go along home / now, / Peter, / so I can get started. // ⑥I've a lot of reading / to do!" //

⑦"But / Ms. Carlyle, / is that all? // ⑧Don't you have other things / for me / to do? // ⑨Won't there be letters / to write? // ⑩Business / to take care of? // ⑪People / to telephone? // ⑫Shopping to do?" //

⑬"I have only a few letters / to write / and am still able to write them. // ⑭I have a daughter / to take care of my business / and make my phone calls. // ⑮There are servants / to do the shopping. // ⑯You're going to be here / for one reason, / Peter / ── to keep my company. // ⑰Don't worry, / my boy! // ⑱You'll be enough / with that!" //

⑲That evening, / over a cup of tea / with his friend, / Anne, / he described / what had happened / that afternoon. // ⑳"I don't know / what I've got into," / he said, / laughing. //

㉑"It sounds exciting / to me," / Anne told him. // ㉒"I think / I'd like Ms. Carlyle. // ㉓You're going to have to spend / a lot of time preparing, / though." //

㉔And he did. // ㉕The afternoons with Ms. Carlyle / discussing English Literature / helped him as much as any lecture / he heard / at the university, / but he worked hard. // ㉖In their discussions / Ms. Carlyle insisted on good reasons / with complete details; / she was not satisfied / with half-answers. // ㉗Peter often read far into the night / in order to be able to give proper replies / to her questions. // ㉘Perhaps, / he thought / as he sat / one evening / reading about the times of Richard III, / this is how teaching will be. // ㉙There would be a lot of work / to do, / he decided, / but if all his students were as interested as Ms. Carlyle / he was going to like it. //

📢意味のまとまりに注意して，本文全体を音読しよう。(316 Words)

Words and Phrases	新出単語・表現の意味を調べよう		
volume 名 [vá(:)ljəm] B1	1.	Anne [ǽn]	アン
keep (one's) company	2.	detail 名 [díːteɪl] A2	3.
be satisfied with …	4.	Richard [rítʃərd]	リチャード

A 【Comprehension 1】 Fill in the blanks in Japanese.

要点を整理しよう【思考力・判断力・表現力】

カーライルさんは自分が本を読むために，ピーターに (1.　　　　　) するように促す。	ピーターはカーライルさんに，ほかに自分がすることがないのかたずねる。

カーライルさんは，ピーターにただ (2.　　　　　) になってくれるだけでよいと答える。

その日の (3.　　　　　)，ピーターは友人のアンに午後の出来事を話す。アンは関心を示す。

午後の議論では，カーライルさんは納得のいく (4.　　) を求める。ピーターは夜遅くまで読み込んで準備をする。

ピーターは，自分の生徒がカーライルさんのようであれば，(5.　　　　　) ことが好きになるだろうと考える。

B 【Comprehension 2】 Answer the following questions in English.

本文のポイントについて答えよう【思考力・判断力・表現力】

1. Why did Ms. Carlyle think Peter did not have to do anything for her except for talking about English Literature?

----

2. What did Anne expect Peter to do when she heard his story with Ms. Carlyle?

----

3. Which did Peter find more meaningful, the afternoons with Ms. Carlyle, or lectures he heard at the university?

C 【Key Sentences】 Translate the following sentences.

重要文について確認しよう【知識・技能】【思考力・判断力・表現力】

⑲ That evening, **over a cup of tea** with his friend, Anne, he described what **had happened** that afternoon.

◆ over a cup of tea で，「お茶を飲みながら」という意味。
◆ 〈had＋過去分詞〉で大過去を表す。述語動詞 described よりも過去であることを表す。
訳 : ----

㉙ There would be a lot of work to do, **he decided**, but **if** all his students **were** as interested as Ms. Carlyle he was going to like it.

◆ decide that ... で「…と結論を出す」。
◆ if-節は仮定法過去。「生徒全員がカーライルさんと同じくらい関心を持っている」状況を想定している。
訳 : ----

Part 5 教科書 p.152 ◁意味のまとまりに注意して，本文全体を聞こう。◎2-46

①The following spring / Peter Brent finished his studies / and graduated / from the university, / with honors. // ②There was Ms. Carlyle / to thank for much / of it. // ③He never would have done / so well, / had she not made him study. //

④The day before he was to leave the university / Peter went to say good-bye / to Ms. Carlyle, / now his very good friend. //

⑤"I will miss you, / Peter," / she told him. // ⑥"These hours with you / each afternoon / have been wonderful. // ⑦I shall never forget them." //

⑧"But / there'll be more, / Ms. Carlyle. // ⑨I'll be teaching / in a school / only five miles / from here / and to come and see you / from time to time / will be no problem / at all." //

⑩"I know, / and I am glad. // ⑪It won't be quite the same / but it will be nice / to see you / whenever you can come. // ⑫Well, / do you know someone / who can take your place? // ⑬I don't intend / to stop my studies / now, / you know. // ⑭There's still too much / to learn." //

⑮Peter smiled. // ⑯"Is it all right / if it's a woman?" / he asked. //

⑰"Does she know her Literature / as well as you do?" //

⑱"Perhaps / better." // ⑲Peter's face suddenly turned red. //

⑳"But / then I should tell you / that I plan to marry her / when she finishes her studies / next year. // ㉑Her name is Anne Eaton." //

㉒"That's good enough for me." // ㉓Ms. Carlyle turned / and pointed to a small box / on the table. // ㉔"Oh, / I almost forgot. // ㉕That's for you / —— a graduation present." //

㉖The young man picked up the box / and opened it. // ㉗Inside was a gold watch. //

㉘"It was Arthur's," / the old lady said / softly, / "and I want you / to have it. // ㉙When you look at the time / perhaps you'll remember me / and the happy hours / we've spent here / together, / you, / the great writers and I." //

㉚Peter looked at the watch / a long time. // ㉛Then, / turning and smiling at the old lady / in the wheelchair, / he leaned over / and kissed her / on the forehead. // ㉜"Most of all, / I'll have memories / of you," / he said. //

◁意味のまとまりに注意して，本文全体を音読しよう。(388 Words)

Words and Phrases	新出単語・表現の意味を調べよう		
Eaton [íːt(ə)n]	イートン	from time to time	1.
intend to ~	2.	forehead 名 [fɔ́ːrhèd] B1	3.
point to …	4.	lean over	5.

A 【Comprehension 1】 Fill in the blanks in Japanese.

要点を整理しよう【思考力・判断力・表現力】

翌（1.　　　），大学を去る前日に，ピーターはカーライルさんにさようならを言いに来る。

| カーライルさんは，ピーターと過ごした時間を振り返る。 |→| ピーターは，近くの（2.　　　）で教える予定で，今後もときどき会いに来ることを伝える。 |→| カーライルさんは（3.　　　　）を続けたいと思っていて，代わりの人がだれなのかたずねる。 |→|

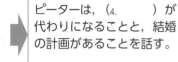

| ピーターは，（4.　　　）が代わりになることと，結婚の計画があることを話す。 |→| カーライルさんは，夫のものだった金色の（5.　　　　　）をピーターに与える。 |→| ピーターはそれを見た後，カーライルさんの（6.　　　）に口づけをする。 |

B 【Comprehension 2】 Answer the following questions in English.

本文のポイントについて答えよう【思考力・判断力・表現力】

1. Why was Peter able to finish his studies and graduate from the university with honors?

　　　　　　　　　　　　　　　　　　　　　　　　　　　　　

2. Why didn't Ms. Carlyle intend to stop her studies?

　　　　　　　　　　　　　　　　　　　　　　　　　　　　　

3. Who originally owned the gold watch?

　　　　　　　　　　　　　　　　　　　　　　　　　　　　　

C 【Key Sentences】 Fill in the blanks and translate the following sentences.

重要文について確認しよう【知識・技能】【思考力・判断力・表現力】

③ He never **would have done** so well, **had she not made him study**.

◆〈would have＋過去分詞〉で「～しただろう」。過去の事実とは異なることを表している。

◆ had she not made him study＝（1.　　[英語1語で]）she（2.　　[英語1語で]）（3.　　[英語1語で]）made him study

訳：　　　　　　　　　　　　　　　　　　　　　　　　　　

⑨ I'll be teaching in a school (only five miles from here) and to come and see you from time to time will be no problem at all.

◆ only five miles from here が直前の a school を修飾している。

◆ and より後は，to come and see you from time to time が主語，will be が動詞。

訳：

Part 1 教科書 p.156 🔊意味のまとまりに注意して，本文全体を聞こう。 ◉2-48

①Jake Belknap found an old desk / in a secondhand store / near his apartment / one Saturday afternoon. // ②The desk came / from an old house / built in the middle of the nineteenth century / in Brooklyn. //

③I never wondered / or cared / who might have used it / long ago. // ④I bought it / because it was cheap. //

⑤I'm twenty-four years old, / and I live in Brooklyn / and work in Manhattan. // ⑥I bring work home / from the office / once in a while. // ⑦And every couple of weeks / or so / I write a letter / to my folks / in Florida. // ⑧So I'd been needing a desk. //

⑨The desk was made of heavy wood. // ⑩At the back of it / rose little compartments / about two feet / above the desktop. // ⑪Underneath them / was a row of three little drawers. //

⑫On that night, / after working for a while / at the desk, / I pulled out one of the drawers / and held it up / in my hand, / admiring its construction. // ⑬And then / it suddenly occurred / to me / that the little drawer / in my hand / was only six inches deep, / while the top of the desk extended / at least / a foot back. //

⑭I pushed my hand / into the opening / and could feel the handle / of a secret drawer / hidden in the back. // ⑮I pulled it out. //

⑯There was some plain white writing paper, / three or four blank envelopes, / a small round glass bottle / of ink, / and a plain black wooden pen. // ⑰I saw / that one of the envelopes was slightly thicker / than the others. // ⑱I opened it / and found a letter / inside. // ⑲Even before I saw the date, / I knew / this letter was *old*. // ⑳The handwriting was beautifully clear, / the letters elegant and perfectly formed. // ㉑The ink was rust-black, / the date / at the top of the page was May 14, 1882, / and reading it, / I saw that it was a love letter. // ㉒It began: //

㉓Dearest! // ㉔Mother, / Father, / and Willy / have long since retired to sleep. // ㉕Now, / the night far advanced, / the house silent, / I alone remain awake, / at last free to speak / to you / as I choose. // ㉖Yes, / I am willing to say it! // ㉗I long for the tender warmth / of your look! //

🔊意味のまとまりに注意して，本文全体を音読しよう。（325 Words）

Words and Phrases 新出単語・表現の意味を調べよう			
Jake Belknap [dʒéɪk bélknəp]	ジェイク・ベルクナップ	secondhand 形 [sèk(ə)n(d)hǽnd] B1	1.
apartment 名 [əpɑ́ːʳtmənt] A2	2.	Manhattan [mænhǽt(ə)n]	マンハッタン
once in a while	3.	Florida [flɔ́ːrɪdə]	フロリダ

compartment 名 [kəmpáːrtmənt]	4.	desktop 名 [désktà(ː)p] B2	5.
underneath 前 [ʌndərníːθ] B1	6.	a row of …	7.
drawer 名 [drɔ́ːər] A2	8.	admire 動 [ədmáɪər] A2	9.
occur to …	10.	envelope 名 [énvəlòup] A2	11.
handwriting 名 [hǽndràɪtɪŋ] B1	12.	elegant 形 [élɪg(ə)nt] B2	13.
rust 名 [rʌ́st]	14.	Willy [wíli]	ウィリー
retire 動 [rɪtáɪər] A2	15.	willing 形 [wílɪŋ] B2	16.
be willing to 〜	17.	long for …	18.
tender 形 [téndər] B2	19.	warmth 名 [wɔ́ːrmθ] B1	20.

A 【Comprehension】 Fill in the blanks in Japanese.

要点を整理しよう【思考力・判断力・表現力】

ジェイク：(1.　　　　) 歳。ブルックリンに住み，マンハッタンで働いている。

古い机：手紙を書くためにジェイクが中古品店で買った。重い (2.　　　　) でできており，(3.　　　) つの引き出しが付いている。

ある夜，ジェイクが引き出しの奥に隠れた引き出しを見つける。

古い手紙：(4.　　　) 年 5 月14日の日付。家族が寝静まり，(5.　　　) に相手への思いを伝えられることを喜ぶ内容で始まっている。

B 【Key Sentences】 Fill in the blank and translate the following sentences.

重要文について確認しよう【知識・技能】【思考力・判断力・表現力】

⑩ **At the back of it** <u>rose</u> <u>little compartments</u> about two feet above the desktop.
　◆場所を表す副詞句を文頭に出して，その後を「動詞＋主語」の語順に倒置している。
　◆動詞 rose の原形は (1.　　　　　　[英語1語で]) で，「高く伸びている」という意味。
　訳 :

㉕ Now, **the night** (being) **far advanced**, **the house** (being) **silent**, I alone remain awake, at last free to speak to you as I choose.
　◆分詞の主語を残した独立分詞構文。being が省略されていると考えるとよい。
　訳 :

Part 2 教科書 p.158 　◁意味のまとまりに注意して，本文全体を聞こう。　◉2-50

①I smiled a little. // ②People once expressed themselves / using elaborate phrases / like these. // ③But I wondered / why it had never been sent. //

④Dear one: / I have to marry a man / I do not love. // ⑤To please my father / I have tried / and sadly I know / I have the duty / to obey / and must accept soon. //

⑥If only you could save me / from that! // ⑦But you cannot / —— for you exist only in my mind. // ⑧But / though you live only in my imagination, / and though I shall never see your like, / you are more dear to me / than the man / to whom I am engaged. //

⑨I think of you / constantly. // ⑩I dream of you. // ⑪I speak with you / —— in my mind and heart. // ⑫If only you existed / outside them! // ⑬Sweetheart, / good night. // ⑭Dream of me, / too. // ⑮With all my love, / I am, // ⑯your Helen //

⑰At the bottom of the page / was written, / "Miss Helen Elizabeth Worley, / 972 Brock Place, / Brooklyn, / New York." //

⑱I was no longer smiling / at this cry / from the heart / in the middle of a long-ago night. // ⑲As I read her words, / she seemed alive / and real to me. // ⑳ And my heart went out / to her / as I stared down at her secret, / hopeless appeal / against the world and time / she lived in. //

㉑I don't know why, / but in the silence / of that spring night, / it seemed natural enough / to remove the cork / from the old bottle of ink, / pick up the pen beside it, / and then, / spreading a sheet of yellowing old notepaper / on the desk, / to begin to write. // ㉒I felt / that I was communicating / with a still-living young woman / when I wrote: //

㉓Helen: / I have just read the letter / in the secret drawer / of your desk. // ㉔I can't tell / what you might think of me / if there were a way / I could reach you. // ㉕Do the best you can, / Helen Elizabeth Worley, / in the time and place / you are. // ㉖I can't reach you / or help you. // ㉗But I'll think of you. // ㉘And maybe I'll dream of you, / too. // ㉙Yours, / Jake Belknap //

◁意味のまとまりに注意して，本文全体を音読しよう。（347 Words）

Words and Phrases	新出単語・表現の意味を調べよう		
elaborate 形 [ɪlǽb(ə)rət]	1.	obey 動 [oʊbéɪ] B2	2.
accept 動 [əksépt] A2	3.	if only …	4.
imagination 名 [ɪmæ̀dʒɪnéɪʃ(ə)n] A2	5.	be engaged to …	6.
dream of …	7.	sweetheart 名 [swíːthɑ̀ːrt] A2	8.

Helen Elizabeth Worley [hélən ɪlízəbəθ wɔ́ːrli]	ヘレン・エリザベス・ウォーリー	at the bottom of …	9.
Brock [brɑ́(ː)k]	ブロック	hopeless 形 [hóupləs] B1	10.
remove A from B	11.	cork 名 [kɔ́ːrk]	12.
notepaper 名 [nóutpèɪpər]	13.		

A 【Comprehension 1】 Fill in the blanks in Japanese.

要点を整理しよう【思考力・判断力・表現力】

手紙の続き：(1.) に従って，愛していない男性と結婚する境遇にあり，(2.) の中の存在である手紙の相手が助けてくれることを願っている。最後にヘレンという名前とニューヨーク・ブルックリンの (3.) が書かれている。

→

ジェイクは，ヘレンが生きていて（4. ）の存在に思えて，返信を書く。

↓

ジェイクの返信：引き出しにあった手紙を読んだことを伝えたうえで，ヘレンが今いる（5. ）と場所でできるかぎり最善を尽くすように励ましている。

B 【Comprehension 2】 Answer the following questions in English.

本文のポイントについて答えよう【思考力・判断力・表現力】

1. What did Helen have to do when she wrote the letter?

   ----

2. Why did Jake stop smiling after reading Helen's letter?

   ----

3. In the letter, what did Jake want Helen to do?

C 【Key Sentences】 Fill in the blank and translate the following sentences.

重要文について確認しよう【知識・技能】【思考力・判断力・表現力】

③ But I **wondered** [why it **had** never **been sent**].

   ◆ wonder は後ろに wh-節を続けて「…かしらと思う」という意味。
   ◆ why-節の時制は受動態の過去完了。wondered よりも以前のことを表す。
   訳：--------

㉔ I can't tell what you might think of me **if** there **were** a way (**I** could reach you).

   ◆ if-節内の述語動詞が（1. ［英語 1 語で］）であることから仮定法過去。現在の事実とは違う仮定をしている。
   訳：--------

113

Part 3 教科書 p.160 ◁意味のまとまりに注意して，本文全体を聞こう。 ◉2-52

①Maybe / what I did seems foolish. // ②It's hard to explain. // ③Still, / I folded the paper, / put it / into one of the old envelopes, / and sealed it. // ④Then / I wrote / "Ms. Helen Worley" / and her address / on the face of the envelope. // ⑤I put an old stamp / on it, / picked it up, / and walked out of my apartment / into the darkness of the night, / heading for the Wister Post Office, / one of the oldest post offices / in Brooklyn, / built, / I suppose, / not much after the Civil War. //

⑥I was extremely busy / all the next week. // ⑦That Friday evening / I worked at home, / sitting at my desk. // ⑧But once more now, / Helen Elizabeth Worley was in my mind. // ⑨I worked steadily / all evening, / and it was around twelve-thirty / when I finished. // ⑩I opened the little center drawer of the desk / into which I'd put some rubber bands / and paper clips. // ⑪And then / I realized / suddenly / that *it* too, / of course, / must have a secret drawer / behind it. //

⑫I hadn't thought of that. // ⑬It simply hadn't occurred to me / the week before. // ⑭And I'd been too busy all week / to think of it / since. // ⑮But now / I pulled the center drawer / all the way out, / reached in, / and touched the little handle there. // ⑯I pulled out the second secret drawer / and there / I found another letter / in rust-black ink / on yellowing old paper. // ⑰It read: /

Please, / oh, please / —— who are you? // ⑱Where can I reach you? // ⑲Your letter arrived / today. // ⑳I cannot conceive / how you saw my letter / in its secret place, / but since you did, / perhaps you will see this one / too. // ㉑Oh, / tell me / your letter is no trick / or cruel joke! // ㉒If I now address someone / who has truly responded / to my most secret hopes / —— do not for a moment longer keep me ignorant / of who and where you are. //

㉓I must hear from you / again. // ㉔I shall not rest / until I do. // ㉕I remain, / most sincerely, / Helen Elizabeth Worley //

◁意味のまとまりに注意して，本文全体を音読しよう。(332 Words)

Words and Phrases 新出単語・表現の意味を調べよう			
foolish 形 [fúːlɪʃ] B1	1.	fold 動 [fóʊld] B1	2.
Wister [wístər]	ウィスター	steadily 副 [stédɪli] B1	3.
rubber 名 [rʌ́bər] B1	4.	conceive 動 [kənsíːv] B2	5.
cruel 形 [krúːəl] B1	6.	ignorant 形 [íɡn(ə)r(ə)nt] B2	7.
hear from …	8.		

A 【Comprehension 1】 Fill in the blanks in Japanese.

夜中，ジェイクは自分がヘレンに書いた手紙を<u>郵便局に出しに行く</u>。　＝
ブルックリンで最も
(1.　　　　　) 郵便局
のひとつ

→

翌週，ジェイクは（2.　　　　　）で仕事をしているときにヘレンを思い出す。そして，机の（3.　　　　　）の引き出しの奥に<u>別の隠れた引き出しがある</u>のを見つける。

翌週，ジェイクは（2.　　　　　）で仕事をしているときにヘレンを思い出す。そして，机の（3.　　　　　）の引き出しの奥に別の隠れた引き出しがあるのを見つける。

↓

ヘレンからの２つ目の手紙：ジェイクがだれであって，(4.　　　　　)に連絡すべきか知りたがっている。また, 手紙が (5.　　　　　) や残酷な冗談ではないことを願っている。

B 【Comprehension 2】 Answer the following questions in English.

1. How was the Wister Post Office distinguished from most other post offices in Brooklyn?

2. What had Jake put in the center drawer of the desk?

3. What concern did Helen express about the letter she had received?

C 【Key Sentences】 Fill in the blank and translate the following sentences.

⑩ I opened <u>the little center drawer of the desk</u> (**into which I'd** put some rubber bands and paper clips).
　◆ put A into B で「A を B に入れる」という意味。前置詞 into は関係代名詞 which の前にある。
　◆ I'd は I (1.　　　　　[英語１語で]) の短縮形。
　訳：

㉒ If I now address <u>someone</u> (**who** has truly responded to my most secret hopes) ― do not 〈for a moment longer〉 **keep** <u>me</u> <u>ignorant</u> of [who and where you are].
　◆文の後半は do not を使った命令文。for a moment longer（もうこれ以上長い間）が挿入されている。
　◆ keep＋O＋C で「O を C のままにしておく」。ignorant of ... は「…を知らない」という意味。
　訳：

Part 4 教科書 p.162 ◁意味のまとまりに注意して，本文全体を聞こう。 ◎2-54

①After a long time, / I opened the first little drawer / of the old desk, / and took out the pen and ink / I'd found there / and a sheet of the notepaper. //

②For minutes, / with the pen in my hand, / I sat there / staring down at the empty paper. // ③Finally, / I dipped the pen into the old ink / and wrote: /

Helen, / my dear: / I don't know / how to say this, / but I do exist, / here / in Brooklyn, / less than three blocks / from where you now read this / —— in the year 1994. // ④We are separated / not by space / but by the years / that lie between us. // ⑤Now / I own the desk / that you once had / and at which you wrote the note I found / in it. // ⑥Helen, / all I can tell you is / that I answered that note, / mailed it / late at night / at the old Wister Post Office, / and that it somehow reached you, / as I hope / this will too. //

⑦This is no trick! // ⑧Can you imagine anyone playing a trick / that cruel? // ⑨You must believe me. // ⑩I live. // ⑪I exist, / 112 years after you read this, / and with the feeling / that I have fallen in love / with you. //

⑫I sat for some time / staring at the wall, / trying to figure out / how to explain something / I was certain / was true. // ⑬Then / I wrote: //

⑭Helen: / There are three secret drawers / in our desk. // ⑮Into the first / you put only the letter / I found. // ⑯Nothing else can now come down to me / in that drawer, / for you cannot now alter / what you have already done. //

⑰Into the second drawer, / you put the note / that lies before me, / which I found / when I opened the drawer / a few minutes ago. // ⑱You put nothing else into it, / and now that, / too, / cannot be changed. //

⑲But / I haven't opened the third drawer, / Helen. // ⑳Not yet! // ㉑It is the last way / you can still reach me, / and the last time. // ㉒I will mail this / as I did before, / then wait. // ㉓In a week / I will open the last drawer. // ㉔Jake Belknap //

◁意味のまとまりに注意して，本文全体を音読しよう。(345 Words)

Words and Phrases	新出単語・表現の意味を調べよう		
dip 動 [díp] B2	1.	play a trick	2.
alter 動 [ɔ́ːltər] B2	3.		

A 【Comprehension 1】 Fill in the blanks in Japanese.

要点を整理しよう【思考力・判断力・表現力】

ジェイクの 2 つ目の返信：
・自分は（1.　　　　　）年，ブルックリンに存在しているが，ヘレンとは隔たりがある。

空間	3 区画に満たないほどの隔たり	時間	(2.　　　　) 年の隔たり

・これはいたずらではない。自分が生きて（3.　　　　　）していることを信じてほしい。
・まだ開けていない 3 つ目の引き出しには特別な意味がある。

1 つ目と 2 つ目	見つけた手紙以外のものはなく，（4.　　　　　）ことはできない。
3 つ目	ヘレンがジェイクに連絡をとることができる（5.　　　　　）のチャンス。

➡ この手紙を出してから 1 週間後に開ける。

B 【Comprehension 2】 Answer the following questions in English.

本文のポイントについて答えよう【思考力・判断力・表現力】

1. What did Jake stare down at before writing the second letter?

2. What feeling toward Helen did Jake express in the letter?

3. When was Jake going to open the last drawer?

C 【Key Sentences】 Fill in the blanks and translate the following sentences.

重要文について確認しよう【知識・技能】【思考力・判断力・表現力】

③ I don't know how to say **this**, but I **do** exist, here in Brooklyn, less than three blocks from [**where** you now read this]

◆ this の内容は「ジェイクが1994年，ここブルックリンにまさに（1.　　　[日本語で]）している」ということ。
◆ do は強調の助動詞。強く発音される。
◆関係副詞 where の先行詞を含む用法。the place where に相当し「…する場所」という意味。

訳：

⑥ Helen, all (I can tell you) is that I answered that note, mailed it late at night at the old Wister Post Office, and **that** it somehow reached you, as I hope this will too.

◆ all (that) I can tell you で，「私があなたに伝えられるすべてのこと」という意味。
◆ this will の後ろには（2.　　　　　[英語 2 語で]）が省略されている。
◆ that-節を等位接続詞で並列する場合，最初の that は省略できるが，後の that は省略できない。

訳：

Part 5 教科書 p.164 ◀意味のまとまりに注意して，本文全体を聞こう。 ◎2-56

①It was a long week. // ②I was terribly tempted / to open the third secret drawer earlier, / but I wasn't sure, / and I waited. //

③Then, / late at night, / a week to the hour / after I'd mailed my second letter / at the old Wister Post Office, / I pulled it out. // ④I'd expected a very long letter, / of many pages, / and full of everything / she wanted to say. // ⑤But there was no letter / at all. // ⑥There was only a photograph, / about three inches square, / faded brown in color. // ⑦The photograph showed a beautiful young woman / in a high-necked dark dress. //

⑧Across the bottom of her photograph / she had written, / "I shall never forget you." // ⑨And as I sat there / at the old desk, / staring at / what she had written, / I understood that, / of course / that was the last time, / as she knew, / that she'd ever be able to reach me. //

⑩It wasn't the last time, / though. // ⑪There was one final way / for Helen Worley / to communicate with me / over the years, / and it took me / a long time, / as it must have taken her, / to realize it. //

⑫Only a week ago, / after much searching, / I finally found it. // ⑬I found the old headstone / in the cemetery, / among the others stretching off / in rows / under the quiet trees. // ⑭And then / I read the inscription / carved into the weathered old stone: / *Helen Elizabeth Worley* / —— *1861-1934.* // ⑮Under this / were the words, / "I NEVER FORGOT." //

⑯And neither will I. //

◀意味のまとまりに注意して，本文全体を音読しよう。（243 Words）

Words and Phrases 新出単語・表現の意味を調べよう			
tempt 動 [tém(p)t] B1	1.	be tempted to ～	2.
headstone 名 [hédstòun]	3.	cemetery 名 [sémətèri] B2	4.
stretch off	5.	inscription 名 [ɪnskrípʃ(ə)n] B1	6.

A 【Comprehension 1】 Fill in the blanks in Japanese.

要点を整理しよう【思考力・判断力・表現力】

（1.　　　　　　　）後，ジェイクは３つ目の引き出しを開ける。

↓

１枚の写真：黒っぽい色のドレスを着た女性。写真の下に「私はあなたを決して忘れないでしょう」とある。

↓

ジェイクは，ヘレンが連絡をとることができる（2.　　　　　　）の時と理解する。

→

数年後，（3.　　　　　　　）にて，ジェイクは静かな木々の下で古い（4.　　　　　　　）を見つける。

↓

墓碑銘：ヘレンの名前，生没年とともに，「決して（5.　　　　　　）なかった」との言葉が刻まれている。

B 【Comprehension 2】 Answer the following questions in English.

本文のポイントについて答えよう【思考力・判断力・表現力】

1. Who was in the photograph Jake found in the third secret drawer?

　...

2. What had Helen written across the bottom of her photograph?

　...

3. What message did Jake find on Helen's headstone?

　...

C 【Key Sentences】 Fill in the blanks and translate the following sentences.

重要文について確認しよう【知識・技能】【思考力・判断力・表現力】

③ Then, late at night, a week **to the hour** after I'd mailed my second letter at the old Wister Post Office, I pulled **it** out.

　◆ to the hour は「ちょうど時間どおり」という意味。

　◆ it ＝（1.　　　　　　　　　　　[英語４語で]）

　訳：...

　...

⑯ And **neither will I**.

　◆〈neither＋助動詞＋主語〉で「…も～しない」。

　◆この文を別の表現にすると，"And I won't（2.　　　　　[英語１語で]）, either." と言いかえられる。

　訳：...

訂正情報配信サイト 14160-01
利用に際しては，一般に，通信料が発生します。

https://dg-w.jp/f/c20d7

CREATIVE English Communication Ⅲ

予習・授業ノート

2024年1月10日　初版　第1刷発行 　編　者　第一学習社編集部
　　　　　　　　　　　　　　　　　　発行者　松本洋介
　　　　　　　　　　　　　　　　　　発行所　株式会社　第一学習社

広島：〒733-8521　広島市西区横川新町7番14号　☎082-234-6800
東京：〒113-0021　東京都文京区本駒込5丁目16番7号　☎03-5834-2530
大阪：〒564-0052　吹田市広芝町8番24号　　　　　　☎06-6380-1391

札　幌☎011-811-1848　　仙　台☎022-271-5313　　新　潟☎025-290-6077
つくば☎029-853-1080　　横　浜☎045-953-6191　　名古屋☎052-769-1339
神　戸☎078-937-0255　　広　島☎082-222-8565　　福　岡☎092-771-1651

書籍コード　14160-01　　　＊落丁・乱丁本はおとりかえいたします。
　　　　　　　　　　　　　　解答は個人のお求めには応じられません。

ISBN978-4-8040-1416-6　　　ホームページ　https://www.daiichi-g.co.jp/